FOREWORD TO THE
SPECIAL PRESERVATION EDITION

If you have never been to the Perryville Battlefield in Kentucky, or have not been for many years, I strongly urge you to go. When you do, be sure to take a younger person with you, because it is one of the best-preserved battlefields in the nation and, therefore, is a place where one can go to learn about what happened there, on the ground where it actually happened. It is an unmatched outdoor classroom. It is an important place to see. If you have been to Perryville recently, then you know exactly what I mean.

The generous members of the American Battlefield Trust (through its division of the Civil War Trust) have, over the years, saved more than 1,100 acres of hallowed ground at Perryville. I recall visiting the battlefield with a couple of buddies in the nineties, and being amazed at how little (fewer than 200 acres at that time) of this major battle of the Civil War was preserved. To walk this hallowed ground now, and know that it will be preserved forever, is immensely satisfying.

As I write this foreword, we have a chance to add another significant 128-acre parcel to the battlefield, securing one more piece of the puzzle that will substantially lead to a completely preserved battlefield.

Books like this unique new examination of the 1862 Kentucky Campaign by fellow Trust Color Bearer Larry Peterson are essential to advancing our knowledge of those times, those people, and what they did. But even after reading every book on a battle, there is still nothing like being on the ground, to see what those soldiers saw, walking the wooded paths and open fields as they did, and trying to imagine what it was really like.

We are honored to partner with the University of Tennessee Press to make the Special Preservation Edition of this new work available to our members all across America and to help save even more hallowed ground at Perryville. Please visit our website at https://www.battlefields.org/visit/battlefields/perryville-battlefield for more information about the battle, and learn how you can help save even more of our history.

Thank you for your generous financial support which will help the Trust not only save the current 128-acre tract at Perryville, but continue to completely preserve these important and evocative battlefields all across America for future generations.

With deep gratitude and appreciation,

Jim Lighthizer
President

DECISIONS OF THE
1862 KENTUCKY CAMPAIGN

OTHER BOOKS IN THE COMMAND DECISIONS IN AMERICA'S CIVIL WAR SERIES

DECISIONS
OF THE 1862
KENTUCKY CAMPAIGN

The Twenty-Seven Critical Decisions
That Defined the Operation

Larry Peterson
Maps by Alex Mendoza

COMMAND DECISIONS
IN AMERICA'S CIVIL WAR

The University of Tennessee Press / Knoxville

Library of Congress Cataloging-in-Publication Data

Names: Peterson, Lawrence K., author.
Title: Decisions of the 1862 Kentucky campaign: the twenty-seven critical decisions
that defined the operation / Larry Peterson; maps by Alex Mendoza.
Description: First edition. | Knoxville: The University of Tennessee Press,
[2019] | Series: Command decisions in America's Civil War | Includes
bibliographical references and index. |
Identifiers: LCCN 2018060917 (print) | LCCN 2018061336 (ebook) |
ISBN 9781621905202 (Kindle) | ISBN 9781621905219 (pdf) | ISBN 9781621905196 |
ISBN 9781621905196 (pbk.)
Subjects: LCSH: United States—History—Civil War, 1861–1865—Campaigns. |
Kentucky—History—Civil War, 1861–1865. | Command of troops—Case studies.
Classification: LCC E474.3 (ebook) | LCC E474.3 .P48 2019 (print) | DDC
973.7/469—dc23
LC record available at https://lccn.loc.gov/2018060917

To my wife, Kathleen,
who has tolerated
my being a Civil Warrior:
all my love

CONTENTS

ILLUSTRATIONS

Figures

Maps

PREFACE

The fact that you are even examining this book is encouraging! Few students of the Civil War are familiar with the audacious Kentucky Campaign of 1862, which came close to gaining the Commonwealth of Kentucky for the Confederacy. Though many presumed Kentucky sympathetic to the Southern cause, by early 1862 it was solidly in Unionist hands.. This campaign caused a huge hiccup in the Union's progress toward defeating the Confederacy, and events could have turned out much differently!

My interest in the Kentucky Campaign of 1862 began with research concerning my great-great-grandfather Brig. Gen. Alfred Jefferson Vaughan Jr. While many of us have relatives who served during the Civil War, few people are related to a general officer involved in that conflict. Being a Civil War "addict" from grade school, I made it a goal of mine to determine what role Vaughan played in the fighting. Amidst two other careers, I was fortunate to spend several years as a National Park Service (NPS) ranger, a job that whetted my already strong interest in history. Many years later, I began investigating Vaughan's path throughout his Confederate service. The result of that research was my *Confederate Combat Commander: The Remarkable Life of Brigadier General Alfred J. Vaughan Jr.*, a biography published by the University of Tennessee Press in 2013.[1]

Who was this Vaughan? When war broke out, he raised a company that became Company E of the newly formed Thirteenth Tennessee Infantry. In the ensuing election of regimental officers, he was chosen lieutenant colonel. After the Battle of Belmont and Col. John Wright's election to the Confederate Congress, Vaughan led the regiment at Shiloh, where he captured a battery. Next, Preston Smith's brigade traveled to reinforce Maj. Gen. Edmond Kirby Smith in eastern Tennessee. As a member of this brigade, Vaughan participated in the Kentucky Campaign of 1862, and his involvement piqued my interest in the operations.[2]

Having previously completed books on the critical decisions of the Chattanooga and Atlanta Campaigns, I wanted to delve into the Kentucky Campaign of 1862 to discover how its critical decisions affected Vaughan. I also wanted to learn why that campaign ended so unsuccessfully for the Rebels. This work, the result of my investigations, is not a narrative history of the campaign, and as such, it looks at the root causes that made the military action happen the way it did. Several individuals who altered the course of the campaign made critical decisions. Each choice is examined as to its effect and its potential alternatives. This approach can lead the reader to evaluate other possible outcomes.

What exactly is a critical decision? My criterion is that a critical decision must have shaped not only the events immediately following it but also the conduct of the campaign or battle from that point on. Realize that armies make thousands and thousands of choices daily, most of them in order to carry out some important decisions. Examining the Kentucky Campaign of 1862 reveals some twenty-seven decisions are considered critical enough to determine the events succeeding them. A decision hierarchy might look like this:

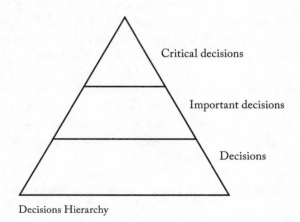

Critical decisions

Important decisions

Decisions

Decisions Hierarchy

Be very careful to not classify a decision that is a reaction to a critical decision as a critical decision itself.

The use of critical decisions allows us to determine why a battle or campaign evolved as it did as opposed to simply recounting what happened. Books describing military action usually mention critical decisions, but they often comingle them with other important choices. Also, these works may not even identify critical decisions as such. This book, however, brings together in one volume all of the critical decisions pertinent to the Kentucky Campaign of 1862.

Readers must also be careful in delineating critical decisions. Our classic demonstration of this process is to ask, What critical decision did Gen. Robert E. Lee make on the third day at the Battle of Gettysburg? The standard response is Pickett's Charge, but, in fact, this is incorrect. Lee had three choices on July 3: he could attack, defend, or retreat. He chose to attack, resulting in the infamous Pickett-Pettigrew-Trimble assault.

Whether these decisions proved good or bad depends on many points of view. One of the most important aspects of studying history is the concept of looking at events from the perspective of their unique historical time frames. Past actions should not be evaluated based on what we know today. We must examine decisions within the context of the time in which they were made. Thus we must be very careful not to factor in our prejudice when considering these choices. The critical decisions aren't viewed as good or bad, but they are examined in hindsight as to their eventual influence on the outcome of the Kentucky Campaign.

Six categories of critical decisions may be found in a battle or campaign: strategic, tactical, organizational, operational, logistical, and personnel. While commanders at all levels may make these choices, individuals at the higher levels of command are the ones who typically do so. Additionally, the critical decisions are grouped into three general periods: the campaign's formation, the campaign itself, and the retreat from Kentucky. The actual campaign is broken into time periods before and after the Battle of Richmond, Kentucky, and the Battle of Perryville, Kentucky. In the interest of keeping things straightforward, the decisions are presented chronologically.

Following is the list of the time frames and critical decisions addressed in each chapter:

Chapter 1. Before the Campaign, June 9–July 31, 1862
    Halleck Splits Up His Force at Corinth
    Davis Removes Beauregard and Places Bragg in Command
    Davis Places Chattanooga within Kirby Smith's
        Department

Each critical decision is presented in the same format for ease of understanding. First, the decision-maker's circumstances are described for readers. Then the advantages and disadvantages of the logical courses of action are outlined. Based on these available options, the critical decision is then presented. At this point, the results and/or impact of that decision are discussed and evaluated, and an alternate scenario or two are discussed. Readers can independently apply the aforesaid approach to any other battle or campaign in this or any other war.

Better appreciating the where and why of these critical decisions involves being on the ground at or near where they were reached and/or carried out. In some cases, readers may view exactly what the decision-maker was observing. This sight may make the decision seem more logical than a written account would. Therefore, a driving tour is an integral part of this series, allowing readers to put their "boots on the ground" and actually stand where some of these decisions were made. The Kentucky Campaign of 1862 presents a problem in that it covered some one thousand miles of territory. Therefore, the campaign driving tour, which follows discussion of the critical decisions, provides an organized list of locations to visit with driving instructions to each one. Readers are directed to explore as many of these sites as desired. Further, readers will be able to integrate these many locations into an itinerary suitable to their interests and available time.

ACKNOWLEDGMENTS

I would like to acknowledge and thank the following for their help and support in this endeavor. First, I want to recognize the excellent efforts of President Jim Lighthizer and David Duncan of the American Battlefield Trust (formerly the Civil War Trust, now incorporated into this new organization) in preserving Civil War battlefields, including Perryville. I urge all readers to join and support this incredible organization (www.battlefields.org). Kurt Holman, the Perryville Battlefield park manager for so many years until his recent retirement, reviewed my work and made several good suggestions, especially concerning Gilbert. Likewise, special thanks to acting park manager Joni House for reading and correcting the manuscript. Thanks to Wayne Basconi, longtime friend and recently member of the Perryville Battlefield Commission for his many hours spent with me on the battlefield. Thanks also to the Battle of Richmond Association and Phillip Seyfrit, Paul Rominger, and Robert Moody for their support. Thanks to the University of Tennessee Press, without whose help, resources, and special relationship, this work would not have been completed. Specifically thanks to Director Scot Danforth, Acquisitions Editor Thomas Wells, and Jon Boggs, Linsey Perry, Stephanie Thompson, Tom Post, and the staff. Matt Spruill, whose collaboration not only on this book, but the entire series, has been crucial to its success. Finally, thanks once again to my wife Kathleen for her continued supporting of my attempts to learn more about the Civil War.

Larry Peterson
Evergreen, Colorado

INTRODUCTION

The Civil War began with the shelling of Fort Sumter in Charleston Harbor in April 1861. Both sides, believing the war would be of short duration, hastily assembled armies. Prodded by President Abraham Lincoln, the field commander of the Union army, Maj. Gen. Irwin McDowell planned, fought, and was defeated at Bull Run or Manassas Junction on July 21, 1861. Both sides settled down after that battle, raising and training their respective armies. In 1862 Maj. Gen. George B. McClellan, now in command of the Union forces, planned and attempted to carry out his Peninsula Campaign. His efforts failed partly due to logistics, McClellan's timidity, and Confederate general Robert E. Lee's tenacity. McClellan retreated from the Richmond areas as a result of the Seven Days' Battles. Lee soundly defeated Maj. Gen. John Pope's army at the Second Battle of Manassas (or Bull Run) and then invaded Maryland, which culminated in the Battle of Antietam on September 17, 1862. Lee then withdrew back into Virginia.

In the Western Theater, the Commonwealth of Kentucky was highly desired by both sides for its capability to provide munificent supplies. For the Union, the protection provided for the Ohio River would prove to be an extremely important supply corridor. For the Confederacy, the Commonwealth would offer a natural boundary. Political factions worked hard to maintain control of Kentucky for their side. However, Kentucky officially declared itself neutral in the war.

On September 4, 1861, Maj. Gen. Leonidas Polk, who believed the defensive location of utmost importance to the Confederacy, captured Columbus,

Kentucky, destroying the Commonwealth's ordered neutrality. Brig. Gen. Ulysses S. Grant immediately captured Paducah, Kentucky, for the Union. The Confederacy then established a defensive line running some four hundred miles through Kentucky, from Columbus through Bowling Green to the Appalachian Mountains. On November 7, Grant attacked the small Confederate force at Belmont, Missouri, immediately across the river from Columbus. Polk sent reinforcements that eventually repulsed the Union general.

On January 19, 1862, Union Maj. Gen. George Thomas defeated an attack by Confederate Brig. Gen. Felix Zollicoffer at the Battle of Mill Springs in eastern Kentucky, which began the collapse of the Kentucky Rebel line. This line fully collapsed when Maj. Gen. Henry Halleck ordered Grant to capture Fort Henry, which guarded the Tennessee River in northern Tennessee. With the help of Adm. Henry Foote and his gunboats, Grant easily captured Fort Henry on February 3, 1862. Not pausing, Grant then moved to nearby Fort Donelson, which guarded the Cumberland River. After several days of navel and land attacks and a Confederate command debacle, Grant captured Fort Donelson and imprisoned some thirteen thousand to fifteen thousand Confederates.

The capture of these two western forts proved hugely significant. Grant had demonstrated that, whatever else he might be, he was a fighter. Once in control of the forts, Union troops could access rivers running deep into the Confederate Heartland. Soldiers navigated the waters with gunboats and transports, and no other Confederate defenses opposed them. Perhaps more significant was the fact that the Rebel defensive line Gen. Albert S. Johnston had established between eastern Kentucky and Columbus had now been broken. While fighting in the East remained essentially a stalemate, the Confederacy was rapidly losing much of its extremely valuable Heartland in the West. Johnston thus retreated deeper into the South. He began concentrating Confederate soldiers at Corinth, Mississippi, and he called on the Confederate government for assistance. Reinforcements arrived from throughout the South.

Grant began taking advantage of the river access and sent Brig. Gen. William T. Sherman upriver (south) to create havoc. Although the Tennessee River was in flood stage, rendering much of the surrounding area inaccessible, Sherman found some high ground at a location named Pittsburg Landing, and Grant began assembling his forces here. Halleck, now in command of most of the Union West, ordered Maj. Gen. Don Carlos Buell and his Army of the Ohio to march from Nashville and reinforce Grant's Army of the Tennessee at Pittsburg Landing. The next objective for Halleck/Grant/Buell was Corinth, where the Memphis and Charleston Railroad crossed the Mobile and Ohio Railroad. This crossing provided an outstanding logistical site where men and supplies could be routed and rerouted to virtually any-where within the Confederacy. This objective was quite obvious to Johnston, who began devising a way to protect it.

Johnston had succeeded and obtained considerable reinforcements: Maj. Gen. Braxton Bragg's troops from Mobile and Pensacola, Polk's troops from Columbus, Gen. P. G. T. Beauregard's from Tennessee, as well as troops from New Orleans and other places in the South. Maj. Gen. Earl Van Dorn's army in Arkansas was also ordered to concentrate in Corinth. Van Dorn refused to cooperate due to nearby Union forces, but had his army joined Johnston's, the results might have been quite different.

Johnston and Beauregard realized that if they could attack Grant's army at Pittsburg Landing before Buell reinforced it, the Confederacy would have a unique opportunity to defeat Federal forces and recapture some of the Heart-land. Seizing this plan, they advanced on Pittsburg Landing. After many dif-ficulties in marching with mostly green troops who had not yet "seen the ele-phant," Johnston finally had his men, divided into four corps, ready to attack early on the morning of April 6, 1862.

At this point in the war, troops were not yet in the habit of building trenches for defense; the Union divisions present at Pittsburg Landing had almost none. Sherman, located farthest from the landing, foresaw very little likelihood of being attacked, and Grant apparently felt the same way. Thus, when the attack began early on the sixth, Sherman's and the other Union divisions were quickly put to flight. The fighting surged past a small log building named Shiloh Church, from which the battle received its name (an alternate name is the Battle of Pittsburg Landing). Although Johnston was mortally wounded, the Confederate onslaught pushed the Union line back toward the landing by late afternoon. After intense fighting at such locations as the "Hornet's Nest," Grant established a final defensive line running west from the landing, fortified with artillery. Due to command confusion and separation, and to the late hour, Beauregard, now in command, called off the fighting for the day. He and his men felt that the next day would result in a great Confederate victory.

However, that was not to be. Grant prepared to go on the attack rather than retreat. During the evening, the first of Buell's divisions reinforced him, as well as Maj. Gen. Lew Wallace's division (Wallace was the eventual author of *Ben Hur*). Before the tired and worn-out Confederates knew what was hap-pening, the Union counterattack began the next morning and pushed them off the battlefield. The Confederates retreated in the rain back to Corinth.

The combined Union force set the stage for the next movement. Dis-pleased when Grant was surprised at Shiloh, Halleck took over command of the two Union armies, relegating Grant to the relatively meaningless position of second-in-command. Halleck, joined with Maj. Gen. John Pope's army, which had just captured New Madrid, Missouri, and Island Number Ten, which allowed Union naval access farther south on the Mississippi River toward Memphis, in the effort to eventually control the river, now began an extremely cautious advance toward Corinth. Moving at the average rate of five hundred yards per day and entrenching every night, it took the troops many days to arrive at the edge of Corinth, where the Confederates were dug in. Grant's assignment and the lack of progress disgusted him. He almost left the army until Sherman talked him into staying.

It was obvious to Beauregard and his commanders that with the odds approximately two to one, the Confederate forces at Corinth could not successfully remain or have much chance of defeating the Union horde in front of them. The lack of potable water for Southern soldiers compounded the problem. In fact, at times a third or more of the Confederates were simply too sick to fight. Left with only one real option, the Rebel force at Corinth conducted an excellent stealthy retreat on the night of May 29. Halleck and his men were caught completely by surprise, and the Union quickly captured Corinth. The Confederates retreated some fifty-two miles south to Tupelo, reaching it on June 9. Van Dorn's and Maj. Gen. Sterling Price's armies joined Beauregard there. These are the positions of the Union and Confederate forces as events resulting in the 1862 Kentucky Campaign commenced.

The Confederates had been driven out of Kentucky with the resulting loss of supplies. From a strategic viewpoint, Kentucky was critical to both sides. Lincoln reputedly exclaimed, "I think to lose Kentucky is nearly the same as to lose the whole game." As readers will discover, many southerners believed that Kentucky was ripe for relief from northern control, and many of its citizens would quickly support the Confederacy if only given an opportunity to do so.[1]

CHAPTER 1

BEFORE THE CAMPAIGN,
JUNE 9–JULY 31, 1862

If you have bypassed the preface, please direct your attention there and read the definition of a critical decision in order to more fully understand the discussions in this book.

Six critical decisions preceded and formed the Kentucky Campaign of 1862. Commanders on both sides made tactical and strategic choices that influenced the resulting campaign. Confederate president Jefferson Davis made a personnel critical decision as well as a particularly important organizational critical decision.

Halleck Splits Up His Force at Corinth

Situation

After the Battle of Shiloh, Halleck's combined armies were roughly twice as large as the Confederate army. As Halleck slowly advanced to Corinth, the Confederates had no choice but to abandon that town. Unopposed, Halleck and his combined armies took possession of Corinth on May 30.

After Johnson had fallen on the first day of fighting at Shiloh, the Rebel army, now under the command of Gen. P. G. T. Beauregard, was forced to retreat south to Tupelo, Mississippi, where it regrouped and refitted. Union

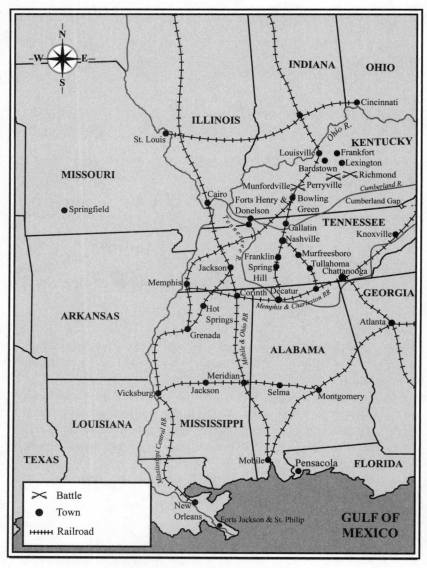

The Western Theater in 1862

forces now had possession of much of Tennessee and northern Mississippi. In fact, the new Confederate line at Tupelo was some 160 miles south of the original Confederate line that had run through Columbus, Kentucky, to Bowling Green. The Confederacy had lost about fifteen thousand square miles of territory.[1]

Despite the capture of Corinth, the affected railroads still ran along parts of their routes, continuing to support Confederate operations. The Federal navy had captured New Orleans in late April, and quickly cleared some four hundred miles of the Mississippi River, up to where the Rebels commanded it near Vicksburg, not allowing Union boat traffic to pass by it. Union forces had captured Memphis on June 6, and Vicksburg and Port Hudson had become the last remaining hindrance to Union traffic along the Mississippi. Capturing the Mississippi River was an integral part of the Anaconda Plan developed by Maj. Gen. Winfield Scott, initially the Union general-in-chief.[2]

Although holding on to Confederate territory was significant, defeating Rebel armies was a more proper course for ensuring the South's defeat. There was never a guarantee that the areas Federal forces held could not be recaptured.

From early in the war president Lincoln favored the redemption of East Tennessee to free supporters of the Union residing there. Buell and other Union generals consistently refused to consider operations there because of poor logistics.

With Corinth in Union hands, another strategic target appeared to be Chattanooga. As the intersection of four railroads, that city was even more valuable than Corinth for supplying the Confederacy and transporting its various armies. The Memphis and Charleston Railroad ran east from Memphis through Corinth to Chattanooga. It interchanged at Stevenson, prior to Chattanooga, with the Nashville and Chattanooga Railroad. At Chattanooga, it linked with the Western and Atlantic Railroad, which connected Atlanta with Chattanooga. Also meeting at Chattanooga was the East Tennessee and Georgia Railroad, connecting that city with not only eastern Tennessee, but eventually Virginia. Union control of Chattanooga, an otherwise small, unimportant city, was a tempting objective to those in command.[3]

Options

Resting with his combined armies in Corinth, Halleck had four options. He could advance south to Tupelo and attack the Army of the Mississippi, which had retreated there from Corinth. He could advance toward Vicksburg and capture it. Moreover, Halleck could advance on Chattanooga, utilizing and guarding the Memphis and Charleston Railroad as his supply line, as he

Maj. Gen. Henry W. Halleck, USA. *The Photographic History of the Civil War, Vol. II.*

moved east. Finally, he could split his combined force, moving his armies in different directions.

Option 1

Halleck could march south to Tupelo and attack the Rebel Army of the Mississippi, which had retreated from Corinth. If successful in engaging this army, Halleck could render it ineffective, and if victorious, he could move at will virtually anywhere in the Western Theater. However, the Rebel army could retreat farther south into Mississippi, eluding Halleck and further extending his supply line, which would become more vulnerable to Rebel cavalry. The notorious Mississippi summer heat would probably cripple many of his soldiers.[4]

Option 2

After Corinth's capture, Vicksburg remained a large strategic target, and its seizure would aid in the Union's possession and opening of the Mississippi River. Federal control of the river would virtually cut off supplies to the Confederacy from the Trans-Mississippi West. At the same time, Northern commerce could be reestablished from the mouth of the Ohio all the way south to New Orleans. Halleck believed that Adm. David G. Farragut of the United States Navy would sail north from New Orleans in July. The Western Gunboat Flotilla, commanded by Capt. Charles Davis (acting flag officer), steamed down from recently captured Memphis and they planned to unite at Vicksburg. If these measures resulted in the capture of Vicksburg, Union fortunes in the Western Theater would skyrocket, placing the Confederacy in a dire situation there. Lincoln and his administration considered this a major objective. However, if Halleck chose to advance to Vicksburg he would encounter vicious summer heat and possible attacks by Rebel cavalry, and he would march with his left exposed to the Confederate Army of the Mississippi. Even so, if Halleck were to capture Vicksburg, he would certainly gain Lincoln's esteem.[5]

Option 3

Another target for capture was the major Confederate railroad terminal in Chattanooga, which provided access to all areas of the South. The terminal's capture would disrupt Rebel railroading and force major rerouting of men and supplies to needed areas of the Confederacy. Maintaining a line to send Halleck's troops necessary food, clothing, ammunition, and fodder would require a dependable railroad from either Memphis or Nashville to Chattanooga. Confederate raiders made this requirement problematic.[6]

Option 4

Halleck's final option was to divide his forces in order to allow simultaneous advances in several directions. He needed to protect his lengthy supply line, particularly since the Tennessee River had dropped below navigable depth. Halleck could disperse parts of his armies to protect newly captured Confederate territory, and he could use some of his many soldiers to reinforce other armies in the Western Theater. However, dispersing his men would reduce his ability to crush subsequent Confederate resistance, and Rebel forces might defeat some of Halleck's split forces in detail. An accepted military axiom is to never divide your forces.[7]

Decision

Halleck arguably made his worst choice of the war when he made the critical decision to divide his forces. He sent Buell with four divisions to advance on Chattanooga. By so doing, Halleck reduced his combat effectiveness, favoring future Rebel maneuvering.[8]

Results/Impact

Halleck began to disperse his available armies and split up his command as he attempted to maintain held territory as well as gain additional Confederate territory. He reappointed Maj. Gen. Ulysses S. Grant to command the Army of the Mississippi, which would continue guarding Corinth and the Memphis and Charleston Railroad. In addition, Halleck ordered two divisions under the command of Maj. Gen. William T. Sherman to Memphis, which had been captured after a naval battle. He sent two more divisions, commanded by Maj. Gen. John McClernand, to Jackson, Tennessee. Maj. Gen. John Pope was sent east to take command, initially of the Army of Virginia, after the debacle of the Seven Days' Battles and Maj. Gen. George B. McClellan's retreat down the Virginia Peninsula. As noted, Halleck directed Buell, with four divisions, to advance east along the Memphis and Charleston Railroad toward the important railroad town of Chattanooga. Buell would use the Memphis and Charleston as a supply line (the Tennessee River was becoming unnavigable due to low water). Maj. Gen. Ormsby Mitchell's division already stationed in Huntsville, Alabama., would reinforce Buell. Likewise, Maj. Gen. George H. Thomas, now located at Iuka, Mississippi, was available to reinforce Buell. Halleck also made Brig. Gen. George Morgan's division at Cumberland Gap available to Buell.[9]

With this new set of deployments under way, possibilities opened up for the Confederates situated at Tupelo. Since they were apparently no longer the objective of Halleck's combined forces, they could now make plans of their own. Finally joined by Maj. Gen. Earl Van Dorn's fourteen thousand poorly equipped men, Beauregard now had some fifty thousand effectives. However, as there appeared to be little for the troops to do but wait on Union movement(s), resting and refitting at Tupelo was to their advantage. As mentioned, the Confederates' combined manpower simply was not large enough to defeat Halleck's many divisions.[10]

Years after the fact, many historians consider Halleck's splitting of his immense force the greatest mistake of his career. Attempting to combat the Confederates in several areas simultaneously, he succeeded in none. The division of his superior force gave the Rebel command options otherwise perhaps not available. Shortly after this decision, Halleck was ordered east to become general-in-chief of the Union armies. An interesting quote from a Northern critic read as follows: "Halleck's demonstrated unfitness for his position induced the administration to find a higher position for him. . . . Unable to command successfully one army, he was ordered to Washington to command all the armies." Halleck's split of his forces that led to the Union advance toward Chattanooga gave Gen. Braxton Bragg time to beat Buell's force there and enable the Kentucky Campaign of 1862.[11]

Alternate Scenario

Halleck faced serious problems with supplies, hot weather, and cooperation within the Union high command. Had he kept his soldiers unified and been a more aggressive field commander, an advance on Vicksburg at this time might have quickly effected the city's capture. This decision would have greatly assisted in opening the Mississippi River to commerce from the junction of the Ohio River to New Orleans. In addition, an advance would have sooner cut off the Confederate Trans-Mississippi's ability to send valuable supplies across the Mississippi River for the military's Eastern and Western Departments.

Some historians believe that Halleck's best move would have been advancing his force toward Jackson, Mississippi, and then Vicksburg. Certainly, opening up the Mississippi River to unimpeded river traffic had been a key Union objective ever since the war began. While supplying his men and horses with enough food would have been a daunting task, Halleck might have been able to at least partially live off the land as he traveled. He and his men would have been open to harassment and attacks from Gen. P. G. T. Beauregard on their left flank. However, Halleck simply had too many troops to have been defeated. Likewise, a Confederate attack would likely have resulted in Confederate defeat. By now it should be obvious that Halleck was not an aggressive commander. It would have been uncharacteristic of him to consider such an advance.[12]

Davis Removes Beauregard and Places Bragg in Command

Situation

Gen. P. G. T. Beauregard had been sick even before the Battle of Shiloh. However, he placed duty to his adopted country ahead of his personal health and continued to command until the Confederate armies were safely in Tupelo. Here the army would regroup, recover its health, and appoint new commanders as necessary. On June 15, Beauregard decided to take sick leave for a week to ten days at a well-known resort at Bladon Springs, seventy-five miles north of Mobile. President Jefferson Davis did not like Beauregard and was upset at his retreat from Corinth. Davis considered the general absent without leave (AWOL), and this status gave the Confederate president sufficient provocation to act.[13]

President Jefferson Davis, CSA. *The Photographic History of the Civil War, Vol. IX.*

Options

Davis had three options: he could leave Beauregard in command; he could replace Beauregard with his second-in-command, Gen. Braxton Bragg; or he could appoint another general to command the future Army of Tennessee.[14]

Option 1

Leaving Beauregard in command was not something Davis would prefer to do. However, changing army commanders was always a traumatic decision. After Gen. Albert S. Johnston's death on the first day of the Battle of Shiloh, Beauregard's performance as army commander on the second day of fighting disappointed many, including Davis. The Confederate president found Beauregard's tendency to produce elaborate, largely ridiculous, unachievable strategies unworkable. Yet Davis had few choices to replace Beauregard, who also enjoyed a hero's reputation for his actions at the Battle of Bull Run and had plenty of political support.[15]

Option 2

If Davis were so inclined, a logical replacement for Beauregard was the army's second-in-command, Gen. Braxton Bragg. Bragg was friends with Davis.

He had also successfully turned his well-trained command at Pensacola into perhaps the best of any Rebel organization. Like Davis, Bragg had a talent for organization and tended to be a micromanager. At this time, Bragg looked like a promising replacement.[16]

Option 3

While Davis's third option was replacing Beauregard with someone other than Bragg, he had few choices. Gen. Robert E. Lee was Davis's unproven staff advisor, and he had a less-than-successful record thus far. Gen. Joseph E. Johnston was in command of the Confederate army in Virginia and unavailable. The only other general was Davis's chief of staff, Samuel Cooper, who, at sixty-two years of age, was not a candidate for field service. Perhaps Davis could promote a lieutenant general to command. Though that choice went against his nature, it was nonetheless an option.[17]

Decision

On June 20, Davis appointed Gen. Braxton Bragg as the new commander of the Army of the Mississippi. Being Davis's personal friend never hurt one's chances for important command. Bragg had proven himself an excellent organizer and disciplinarian. However, he had a brusque personality and appeared somewhat sickly to others. After removing Beauregard from command, Davis eventually sent him east to head a much less significant department.[18]

Results/Impact

Only time would tell whether Bragg could plan and execute battles and campaigns. He proved to be a reasonable army commander as long as things went his way, but when events did not follow his script, he seemed unable to move his army to regain control of the situation. This failing would be proven time and time again as the war unfolded. While Bragg lacked ability, he also didn't care to cultivate the favor of his subordinate commanders. These junior officers failed to support him or take the initiative when it was necessary, fearing his retribution if anything went wrong. From early on, Bragg's subordinates, especially Lieut. Gen. Leonidas Polk, conspired to have him removed from command. The general rapidly lost the support of his men, and they despised his cruel discipline.[19]

Bragg's appointment to command this army allowed him to engineer the brilliant Kentucky Campaign of 1862. However, as the fighting unfolded the enemy did not conform to Bragg's predictions, and since large numbers of recruits failed to flock to the Rebel army, his grandiose plans fell through. Bragg was forced to retreat back into Tennessee.[20]

Alternate Scenarios

Had Beauregard been left in command or had another general been appointed instead of Bragg, the Confederate effort in the West likely would not have turned out much different. The only exception would have resulted from Gen. Robert E. Lee's appointment to command in the West. At this time, Lee was still an unproven advisor to Davis. Also, it was too early in the war for some of the Confederacy's more competent senior commanders to have gained the necessary experience and to have demonstrated the leadership ability to re-place Beauregard. Lee would eventually build a solid command led by capable subordinate generals such as Thomas "Stonewall" Jackson, Jubal Early, and James Longstreet. However, a similar structure had not evolved in the West.[21]

Davis Places Chattanooga within Kirby Smith's Department

Situation

President Davis had established a series of departments, each responsible for defending a portion of the Confederacy. This common military practice continues today. The problem with designating departments was that each departmental commander wanted absolute control within his department. Furthermore, most commanders deemed protecting their departments criti-cal to the Confederate cause. They typically did not desire outside command-ers' interference, and there was no incentive for one department commander to assist another. With no motive for cooperation, each department stood on its own.

Maj. Gen. Edmund Kirby Smith had just been appointed commander of the Department of East Tennessee. Kirby Smith had graduated from West Point in 1845 and won the brevets of first lieutenant and captain during the Mexican War. Prior to the Civil War, he had taught at West Point and fought Indians on the Texas frontier. Kirby Smith entered Confederate service as a lieutenant colonel and served initially under Brig. Gen. Joseph E. Johnston in the Shenandoah Valley. Promoted to brigadier general on June 17, 1861, Kirby Smith achieved fame for his performance at the Battle of First Bull Run or Manassas, where he was severely wounded. A grateful Davis promoted him to major general on October 11, 1861. On February 15, 1862, after sufficiently recovering from his wounds, Davis assigned him command of the Depart-ment of East Tennessee.[22]

Maj. Gen. Edmund Kirby Smith, CSA. *The Photographic History of the Civil War, Vol. X.*

Kirby Smith quickly realized that this assignment required defending the territory between Cumberland Gap to the east and Chattanooga to the west; the two locations were some 180 miles apart. To protect his district, he commanded the Army of East Tennessee, which numbered no more than ten thousand poorly armed soldiers. Kirby Smith faced Federal forces advancing against both of his flanks. On July 18, Brig. Gen. George Morgan and his division of ten thousand men captured the Cumberland Gap and posed a threat to Knoxville. Kirby Smith's men badly needed support, and he feared that Buell's advance on Chattanooga could keep Bragg's army from providing it. However, Chattanooga was in Kirby Smith's department. It was his responsibility to protect the city, so he began a campaign to solicit reinforcements for his district by calling on President Davis for assistance.[23]

Options

Davis had three options: He could leave the Department of East Tennessee, including Chattanooga, under the command of Kirby Smith. Alternatively, he could not only keep the Department of East Tennessee separate, but also reinforce it with additional units. Finally, he could establish Kirby Smith's command as a district under Bragg. This last course of action would eliminate future coordination problems, as Kirby Smith would be junior to Bragg.[24]

Option 1

Davis's first option was to keep the Department of East Tennessee under Kirby Smith's command. If implemented, this measure would keep Kirby Smith an independent department commander who reported to Jefferson Davis. While this could eliminate problems of coordination, it would not augment Kirby Smith's small army in its responsibility to defend the department, especially Knoxville, Chattanooga, and the Cumberland Gap.[25]

Option 2

Perhaps a more useful option would be to keep Kirby Smith in command of his district but augment his command with additional troops. Reinforcements would allow him to better defend his department from Union advances. Finding these additional troops would undoubtedly burden Davis, who would have to borrow them from other departments.[26]

Option 3

Davis could designate the Department of East Tennessee as a district under Bragg's command. While this option would place Kirby Smith under the authority of his senior, it would also allow Bragg and his superior numbers to aid in the defense of Chattanooga. The city was an obvious strategic target for the Union. However, Kirby Smith sought independent command and would chafe at being required to take orders from Bragg.[27]

Decision

On June 20, in conjunction with the change of command of the Army of the Mississippi, President Jefferson Davis apparently altered Gen. Braxton Bragg's department boundary to include Chattanooga. Yet Davis confirmed to Kirby Smith that Chattanooga was his responsibility. When Bragg arrived in the city, he was shocked to discover that, according to Davis, it remained within Kirby Smith's separate department. Bragg was now a guest in Chattanooga.[28]

Results/Impact

When Davis made this change, it became problematic for Gen. Braxton Bragg and his Department of the Mississippi. If Bragg were to move to and/or assist Kirby Smith by advancing into Kirby Smith's department, he would be there as a "guest" despite his seniority. Bragg initially believed that Chattanooga was in his department. On July 18, President Davis issued General Orders No. 50 from Richmond, Virginia, to redraw the borders of the two departments and firmly place Chattanooga in Kirby Smith's Department of East Tennessee. On August 6, after Bragg had moved into Smith's department in Chattanooga, he received his copy of this general order. Realizing he was now Kirby Smith's guest, Bragg initially treated him with equal respect and allowed him to set off on his own advance into Kentucky. The result was lost opportunities for Confederate victories, which significantly hurt campaign coordination between Bragg and Smith. Overall, Kirby Smith's avoidance of Bragg in order to maximize his chances at independent command did not help the Rebel cause.[29]

Alternate Scenario

Had Bragg been placed in command over Kirby Smith and his department, or had he simply assumed command based on his higher rank soon after his appointment, the Kentucky Campaign of 1862 might have resulted in better coordination between the Confederacy's Army of the Mississippi and Army of Kentucky. The combined force of Kirby Smith's small army augmenting Bragg's larger one could have directly confronted Buell earlier in the campaign. This could possibly have changed the outcome for the better for Bragg, Kirby Smith, and the Confederacy.

Kirby Smith Decides to Liberate Kentucky

Situation

Brig. Gen. John Hunt Morgan had achieved a reputation for aggressive cavalry operations. His advance into Kentucky, ordered by Kirby Smith, was a continuation of his aggressive raiding style. Morgan had departed Knoxville on July 4, 1862, with some nine-hundred troops and had raided the Kentucky bluegrass, succeeding in three weeks in capturing hundreds of Yankee horses as well as about twelve-hundred prisoners. Morgan further encouraged the soon-to-be labeled "Kentucky Campaign of 1862" with an observation he made to Kirby Smith. On July 16, he notified Kirby Smith by telegram, "The whole country [Kentucky] can be secured, and 25,000 or 30,000 men will join you at once." Likely more than any other cause, this opinion, along with the increase in available troops, motivated Kirby Smith to begin the Kentucky Campaign.[30]

As the war continued, Kirby Smith was anxious to continue reaping glory for himself. He had been given much credit for the Rebel success at the Battle of First Manassas or Bull Run after being wounded there. The Kentucky Campaign was an opportunity for further success for the Confederacy and for himself. Morgan's optimistic report seemed to indicate that Rebel success

Col. John H. Morgan, CSA. *The Photographic History of the Civil War, Vol. VII.*

was very likely, as Kentucky would welcome the chance to escape from Union bondage. Initially the problem was that Kirby Smith did not have enough men to successful defend his department. He faced potential Union invasion both at the eastern edge of his department at Cumberland Gap, as well as at the western boundry at Chattanooga.On May 27, he requested help from the governor of Georgia and the Richmond government, but he received little help. When he and the Richmond government learned of Maj. Gen. Don Carlos Buell's pending advance toward Chattanooga, Kirby Smith finally began to receive reinforcements. These reinforcements gave him options. Seizing on the possible opportunity to invade Kentucky, based on Morgan's promise of additional recruits for the Confederacy, Kirby Smith had to settle upon one of two options if he was to liberate Kentucky.[31]

Options

Kirby Smith had two options to assist him in liberating Kentucky: he could obtain reinforcements for his command and then advance and liberate it on his own, or he could attempt to coerce Bragg into joining his effort.[32]

Option 1

Kirby Smith needed reinforcements to ensure that his small army had a reasonable chance of success in an invasion of Kentucky. Where would these reinforcements come from? With Davis's allocation of manpower into districts and departments, no commander wanted to part with any of his men. Appeals to various entities, including Davis, had gone unheeded.[33]

Option 2

To spearhead an invasion of Kentucky, Bragg's soldiers were a potentially useful resource for Kirby Smith. Bragg indeed had the requisite manpower, and his troops could increase Kirby Smith's numbers and surprise the Yankees. Unfortunately for Kirby Smith, however, Bragg outranked him. In any joint operation under Bragg's direct command, Kirby Smith would lose his independent command—something he was loath to do.[34]

Decision

Kirby Smith made the critical decision to appeal to Bragg for reinforcements. On June 26, Gen. Braxton Bragg sent Kirby Smith Maj. Gen. John McCown's division of about three thousand men. The junior officer's request for assistance finally began to pay off. Eventually Kirby Smith would not only gain enough resources to protect his department, but also invade Kentucky, take an offensive role, and attempt to capture part or all of that state for the Confederacy.[35]

Results/Impact

Had Morgan not sent him such an optimistic report, Kirby Smith might have been much less inclined to advance into Kentucky on his own initiative. Perhaps he would have continued to cooperate with Braxton Bragg in a more coordinated campaign effort. As such, Kirby Smith took Morgan's opinion at full face value and believed that Kentucky was his for the taking. While there would be glory in liberating Kentucky from its Union masters, physically adding the state to the Confederacy would ensure that precious supplies and manpower would flow into the South. This was simply too much of a grand opportunity for Kirby Smith to ignore! As a result, on at least a temporary basis, Kirby Smith ignored the agreement that had been forged with Bragg and moved out on his own.[36]

Kirby Smith and Bragg soon discovered that, despite Kentuckians' celebration of both Rebel armies' arrival, the citizens were not inclined to actually support the Confederacy. This was especially true of Kentucky males, who did not flock to the Confederate colors and enlist in any great number. Instead, these men preferred to remain at home, supporting neither side. Such factors as divided families, slavery, state and national leadership, previous military service, and the commonwealth's past military history all made any decision to join a particular side that much more difficult. Rebel wisdom also believed that these men, rather than rendering service to the Confederacy, preferred to concentrate on their own financial future. This would have a severe negative impact on the Confederacy, and particularly on the Kentucky Campaign of 1862. Kirby Smith had advised Bragg of the wonderful possibilities awaiting them both in Kentucky. Thus Bragg was certainly motivated to forge a movement into that state, appreciating the opportunity to live off its land and augment his army with its men. Had Morgan not sent such a positive message to Kirby Smith, both commanders might have been less likely to advance aggressively into Kentucky. However, they may have cautiously continued their various advances, relying more on their existing manpower and not expecting a surge in new recruits. The reality Bragg and Kirby Smith actually faced might have tempered their optimism.[37]

Alternative Scenario

Had Kirby Smith allowed Bragg to command both of their departments, the resulting effort might well have altered the Kentucky Campaign more in the Confederacy's favor. Combined coordinated attacks at the appropriate time might have allowed Confederate inroads into Kentucky. Regrettably, Kentuckians' lack of enthusiasm for the invading Rebels might have effected little change in the outcome of the campaign.[38]

Bragg Decides to Beat Buell to Chattanooga

Situation

Maj. Gen. Don Carlos Buell graduated from West Point in the notable class of 1841 in which some twenty members became Civil War generals. Buell fought well in the Mexican-American War and was twice brevetted for bravery in that conflict. He served in many departments from the frontier to Washington, D.C. Buell, then ranking as a lieutenant colonel, was serving as adjutant of the Department of the Pacific in San Francisco at the beginning of the Civil War. On May 17, 1861, he was commissioned a brigadier general of volunteers. Shortly thereafter Maj. Gen. George B. McClellan selected Buell to lead the new Army of the Ohio. He eventually led that command to Nashville, and then augmented Grant's beleaguered command at the Battle of Shiloh. After his promotion to major general. on March 22, 1862, Buell was appointed commander of the Department of the Ohio. Many classified him as a micromanager, and President Lincoln accused him of having a case of

Maj. Gen. Don Carlos Buell, USA. *The Photo-graphic History of the Civil War, Vol. X.*

the "slows." Ordered with four divisions to capture Chattanooga, Buell did maneuver slowly.[39]

As noted above, in response to repeated calls for help, Gen. Braxton Bragg sent Kirby Smith Maj. Gen. John McCown's division of about three thousand men on June 26. Kirby Smith's decision to ask for assistance finally began to pay off. The protection of Chattanooga and its Rebel railroad hub was a paramount Confederate objective requiring action. This would figure in the Confederate response to Buell's apparent movement toward that city.[40]

Options

Bragg had three options. He could remain in Tupelo and observe the movements of Buell and other Union forces before committing himself to action. He could pursue Buell as he advanced toward Chattanooga, harassing his troops and attempting to cut his supply line. Lastly, Bragg could attempt to move his army to Chattanooga ahead of Buell.[41]

Option 1

Greatly outnumbered by the combined Union armies, Bragg was not able to attack them head on. Until he became aware of the Union armies' intentions and possible dispersal, his safest action would be to remain in Tupelo while

Gen. Braxton Bragg, CSA. *The Photographic History of the Civil War, Vol. X.*

he continued to rest and refit his army. However, sitting and waiting on the enemy was not really a viable option.[42]

Option 2

Although smaller than the Union force that had seized Corinth, Bragg's army could shadow the Federals as they moved toward Chattanooga, overpowering isolated units. Buell's supply line, the Memphis and Charleston Railroad, would be vulnerable to attack by Bragg. As Buell would have to continuously guard that line, his advance would be slowed.[43]

Option 3

A final option was for Bragg to move his army past Buell's and attempt to arrive in Chattanooga before the enemy. This course of action would provide a strong defense for the city and its railroad hub, which the Confederacy desperately needed to retain. A successful, safe, and efficient transfer would require a tremendous amount of coordination. But after sending McCown's Division to Chattanooga via a roundabout route on June 26, arriving on July 3, Bragg knew that the concept was feasible.[44]

Decision

In an attempt to arrive ahead of Buell, and to protect the city from falling into Federal hands, Bragg ordered his army to Chattanooga.[45]

Results/Impact

Beginning on July 23, Bragg ordered the remaining units of his Army of the Mississippi to Chattanooga. He sent his supply trains and artillery from Tupelo to Chattanooga more directly via roads. This large movement by rail placed a severe burden on the Confederate system, which managed to come through with enough engines and cars to complete the transfer efficiently (for the most part). The circuitous railroad route totaled 776 miles and involved six separate railroads and a ferry trip over Mobile Bay.[46]

Sending troops to Chattanooga had several positive results. First, Bragg was now in a position to prevent Buell from capturing Chattanooga, thus preserving this critical railroad junction. Second, though in a new location, Bragg was still able to keep his army supplied. Third, this movement had the benefit of protecting the west end of Kirby Smith's Department of East Tennessee. Thus Kirby Smith could keep his forces at the eastern end of his department, where they could protect that area from Union invasion. Fourth, Bragg was in a great location to move into central Tennessee and even Kentucky if he desired, confusing the Union high command as to what movements he might actually undertake. However, at this time he was focused on defending the important rail hub.[47]

Alternate Scenario

Had Bragg followed Buell and attempted to cut his supply line, he might have forced Buell to abandon his movement toward Chattanooga. However, Buell and the Union high command would likely have designated additional troops to defend his supply line, perhaps causing a confrontation. In the end, Federal soldiers might still have failed to capture Chattanooga. It appeared to them that Grant might reinforce Buell against the combined movement of Kirby Smith and Bragg. This measure would allow the armies under Price and Van Dorn to open up Western Tennessee, ridding that area of Union forces. If Grant did not move to reinforce Buell, Buell had no choice but to retreat along his line of supply. Either movement would enable the Confederacy to recapture parts of Tennessee.[48]

Bragg and Kirby Smith Agree to Conduct a Joint Campaign

Situation

After Bragg arrived in Chattanooga, he met face-to-face with Kirby Smith on July 31. Closeted in Bragg's hotel headquarters for many hours, the men discussed possible plans to drive the Union forces already in Tennessee out of the state. They also considered advancing into Kentucky and capturing it for the Confederacy. Together, Bragg's reasonably large army and Kirby Smith's small one might cause mischief for the Union forces in Tennessee and Kentucky. Bragg had assumed that Chattanooga was within his department. He was surprised to discover that, in fact, he was now a visitor to Smith's district, as Davis had reaffirmed. Bragg therefore found himself in an uncomfortable situation.[49]

Options

As the ranking officer, Bragg considered three options for movements with Kirby Smith. Bragg could order Kirby Smith to accompany him on a movement into Tennessee and/or Kentucky, even though Kirby Smith technically was an independent department commander. Second, Bragg could allow Kirby Smith to operate entirely at his own discretion within his Department of East Tennessee. At the same time, Bragg could move within his own department. Finally, Bragg could authorize and conduct a joint campaign into Tennessee and Kentucky. The two commands would remain split initially and rejoin somewhere in these two states in the future.[50]

Option 1

Although Bragg significantly outranked Kirby Smith, he was suddenly out of his department. Therefore, Bragg decided to reconsider his command position. His rank presumably gave him the authority to issue orders to Kirby Smith. Adding to the confusion, Kirby Smith said, "[I will] not only cooperate with you [Bragg], but will cheerfully place my command under you subject to your orders." Having a single commander in charge of whatever operation the officers chose would certainly simplify who was to do what. Kirby Smith would have no choice but to carry out Bragg's orders. This would place the responsibility on Bragg. Kirby Smith was not likely to be pleased in the role of second-in-command or in another lesser command assignment.[51]

Option 2

Bragg could maintain the arrangement whereby each commander remained in charge of his department. This was the legal approach, and both men could act as they thought best for their department. The problem with this option was that cooperation between Bragg and Kirby Smith was neither guaranteed nor likely to be maintained as they followed their instincts.[52]

Option 3

The final option was for Bragg and Kirby Smith to cooperate while maintaining their individual commands. While a great compromise, this choice gave Kirby Smith essentially the same level of command as Bragg, who far outranked him. Coupled with Kirby Smith's urge to advance into Kentucky, cooperation would bode ill for Bragg as he and Kirby Smith went their separate ways.[53]

Decision

Based on the appearance of complete agreement, Bragg and Kirby Smith opted to work together on a plan of invasion into Tennessee and Kentucky.[54]

Results/Impact

This decision resulted the agreement that Kirby Smith would initiate an attack against Union Gen. John Morgan's strong position at Cumberland Gap, located north of Knoxville, at the eastern edge of Kirby Smith's department, in order to clear out Union troops from his rear. Meanwhile, Bragg would assemble his arriving supply wagons and artillery, which continued to stream into Chattanooga, in preparation for an advance. If Kirby Smith captured Cumberland Gap, he would join Bragg in Chattanooga. They would then begin a combined movement into Middle Tennessee and possibly Kentucky. The officers' plan, which seemed workable, was to recapture at least some of the Heartland, gain recruits to augment their armies, and force Buell out of the state. To further assist Kirby Smith in his initial efforts, Bragg had also loaned him two of his better brigades under the command of Brig. Gen. Patrick Cleburne. These soldiers would further augment Kirby Smith's command.[55]

However, this joint plan was not without drawbacks. The key provision of the plan was the necessity for both generals' full cooperation. Without this teamwork, the timing of the new campaign would become problematic, and precise timing was seldom achieved during the Civil War. Kirby Smith was required to capture and dispose of George Morgan and his men at Cumberland Gap and then quickly march some two hundred miles west to Chattanooga. Price and Van Dorn would need to accurately conduct simultaneous advances to counter any Union movement to reinforce Buell. These maneuvers would require precise orchestration on the part of the Confederate commanders. However, as we shall see, the proposed joint operation fell apart almost from the beginning.[56]

Alternate Scenario

Had Bragg brought Kirby Smith's army under his own command (possibly requiring Jefferson Davis's approval), these reinforcements would have made Bragg more likely to confront Buell's army in a significant battle to regain at least Middle Tennessee. In this scenario, Bragg would not have allowed Kirby Smith to maneuver on his own. Had Bragg emerged the victor in this battle he might have then advanced into Kentucky, possibly gaining it as a full member of the Confederacy. However, Bragg would likely not have advanced into Kentucky unless he was confident that both Chattanooga and Middle Tennessee were safe. Unfortunately, Kentuckians' lack of interest in serving in the Rebel army, combined with the problem of maintaining adequate supplies, would have ultimately been a detriment to effecting this plan.[57]

CHAPTER 2

THE KENTUCKY CAMPAIGN BEGINS, AUGUST 1–29, 1862

Although Gen. Braxton Bragg and Maj. Gen. Edmund Kirby Smith had agreed on a plan of cooperation, Kirby Smith would quickly abandon his role of capturing Cumberland Gap. He was eager to advance into Kentucky, and he did not want to waste time attempting to force the Union's Brig. Gen. George Morgan out of the gap. Kirby Smith's relinquishment of his agreement with Bragg caused five critical decisions resulting in the Battle of Richmond, Kentucky, and the Battle of Perryville, and directly influencing the rest of the campaign.[1]

Kirby Smith Decides to Bypass Cumberland Gap and March to Lexington

Situation

As previously mentioned, Kirby Smith had been enticed by the telegram he received on July 16 from his cavalry commander, Col. John Hunt Morgan. The colonel reported that Kentucky was ripe for invasion, and its population was simply awaiting a liberator. Kirby Smith quickly had realized that he could be that liberator, winning more glory for himself and further gains for the Confederacy.[2]

As had just been agreed, while Bragg awaited his final troops and supplies, Kirby Smith would move on, invest, and capture Cumberland Gap. The Gap, which Brig. Gen. George Morgan's division had captured on July 16, was an important passageway to the East, and a crucial supply line for the Confederacy passed through it. Morgan's presence there compromised that supply line and also threatened Smith's right or eastern flank. Ignoring Morgan's and his men would place them in position to advance on Kirby Smith. Even before arriving, Kirby Smith knew that it would be next to impossible to capture Cumberland Gap without requiring much time, effort, and loss of manpower. Additionally, Kirby Smith himself faced a lack of supplies in this area to maintain his force, further complicating the issue. A siege could take weeks or more, postponing his advance into Kentucky.[3]

Options

Kirby Smith had two options here: he could follow the joint plan agreed on with Bragg, or he could act on his own and advance into Kentucky.[4]

Option 1

As they had agreed, Bragg expected Kirby Smith to advance to Cumberland Gap and capture it. This plan would eliminate a threatening Union force in Kirby Smith's (and potentially Bragg's) rear. Once this threat was removed, the major general would join forces with Bragg for a movement into Kentucky. The downside to this decision was the fact that capturing a heavily reinforced and well-supplied Union force at the Gap would take time, perhaps a month or longer.[5]

Option 2

Kirby Smith desired the fame and glory of an advance deep into Kentucky to liberate the state for the Confederacy. While a military necessity, a siege at Cumberland Gap would take many weeks to accomplish and be costly in terms of manpower. Kirby Smith's chances for a successful assault on Kentucky might well diminish with time.[6]

Decision

Kirby Smith abandoned his joint plan with Bragg and made the critical decision to advance into Kentucky, bypassing Cumberland Gap. While he was supposed to join Bragg as soon as the Gap was secure, Kirby Smith quickly dismissed that operation. What he did not want to do at this point was waste time attempting to capture Cumberland Gap. Therefore, Kirby Smith wrote

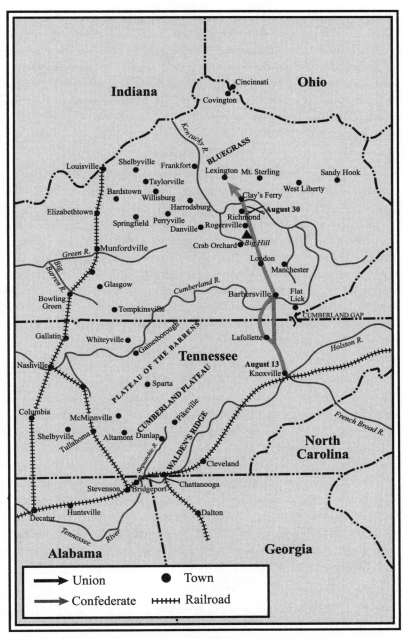

Route of Kirby Smith's Invasion of Kentucky,
August 13 to October 8, 1862

Bragg on August 9 advising him that, due to the supplies available to the be-sieged, it would be too time-consuming to wait on Cumberland Gap's ultimate seizure. Further, Kirby Smith made the excuse that he could not adequately supply his men if he remained near the gap. Therefore, he advocated pursuing more valuable results by moving north into Kentucky, bypassing Morgan's command in order to feed his men. The plan that he and Bragg had carefully contemplated and agreed on was now invalid.[7]

Results/Impact

Though displeased with Kirby Smith's new direction, Bragg felt that he had no direct authority over the junior officer. Writing to Kirby Smith the next day, Bragg, undoubtedly furious at Kirby Smith, advised against his change of movement. In an eventual attempt to rationalize Kirby Smith's sudden abandonment of their agreement, Bragg grudgingly admitted that Lexington might be the better objective. Kirby Smith's sudden change of plans placed new stress on Bragg and his course of action. What should Bragg do? Late on August 13, Kirby Smith began advancing on Cumberland Gap. Having already determined not to invest the Union position there, he deployed Brig. Gen. Carter L. Stevenson's division of some nine thousand men to keep an eye on Morgan's troops.[8]

Alternate Scenario

What might have resulted had Bragg officially ordered Kirby Smith to unite with him in Chattanooga, perhaps under Jefferson Davis's orders? A joint advance might have allowed Bragg to aggressively attack Buell's army in Tennessee. A victory here would have regained Middle Tennessee for the Confederacy. This victory might then have resulted in the successful advance into Kentucky and its possible addition to the Rebel fold. However, in this scenario the Union command would have aggressively recruited additional forces to maintain its hold on Kentucky, necessitating a direct confrontation of the invading Rebels. Even if Bragg were successful in this invasion, as noted above, it would still have been difficult for the Confederacy to keep Kentucky legitimately in the Confederacy.[9]

Kirby Smith Orders Morgan to Compromise Buell's Supply Line

Situation

As discussed previously, Buell's supply line was tenuous at best, as he de-pended mainly on the Memphis and Charleston Railroad to bring supplies from Union-controlled Memphis. As Buell advanced farther east, he would gain access to two new supply lines—the Nashville and Decatur Railroad, which connected with the Memphis and Charleston Railroad at Decatur, Alabama; and the Nashville and Chattanooga Railroad, which also connected with the Memphis and Charleston Railroad farther east at Stephenson, Alabama. The Union forces in northern Mississippi and Alabama received supplies from both railroads, with terminals in Nashville, which, in turn, received supplies from Louisville, Kentucky, via the Louisville and Nashville Railroad. Maintenance of this supply line was critical to the Union efforts to maintain control over Middle Tennessee, Alabama, and northern Mississippi. Federal troops had captured the Confederate capitol at Nashville shortly after Grant had captured Forts Henry and Donelson early in 1862. Disruption of this line could not be tolerated.[10]

The Confederacy quickly recognized the importance of these railroads and continually tried to disrupt their operations. As Kirby Smith began his advance into Kentucky, he had the opportunity to participate in this interference.[11] Brig. Gen. John H. Morgan (not to be confused with the Union's Brig. Gen. George Morgan at Cumberland Gap), operating as an independent command but serving under Kirby Smith, was already operating in the area north of Nashville, Tennessee. His report that Kentucky was ripe for the taking gave Kirby Smith the impetus to propose and order the advance into that state.[12]

Options

As Kirby Smith initiated his invasion, he faced two options concerning Morgan: he could order Morgan to join up with the rest of his cavalry and infantry as this combined force marched toward Lexington, or he could order Morgan to try and sever the Louisville and Nashville Railroad.[13]

Option 1

Kirby Smith could order Morgan to join his own small army, now named the Army of Kentucky. This would provide added protection and reconnaissance as Kirby Smith advanced farther into Kentucky. However, Col. John Scott's cavalry brigade could perform the same services.[14]

Option 2

Kirby Smith's other option was to order Morgan to cut the Louisville and Nashville Railroad to disrupt the flow of Union supplies to Nashville and points south. Since Morgan was already near that railroad, he could quickly target a specific location, ride to it, and commence destroying the tracks.[15]

Decision

Kirby Smith sent Morgan to sever the railroad, and Morgan wasted little time in following his orders.[16]

Results/Impact

On August 12, 1862, Morgan destroyed part of the Louisville and Nashville Railroad just north of Gallatin, Tennessee. He and his men also set fire to the support timbers of the one-thousand-foot-long Big South Tunnel, which would take more than three months to rebuild. Wagons could be used for a time to detour around the ruined tunnel. But this transportation method was much less efficient, and the Union's rate of supply rapidly dwindled. Like-wise, on July 13, Nathan Bedford Forrest, a newly promoted brigadier general, had raided Murfreesboro, Tennessee, and destroyed several nearby Union supply depots, as well as several neighboring bridges of the Nashville and Chattanooga Railroad. Maj. Gen. Don Carlos Buell's supply line was temporarily wrecked.[17]

Once ordered into action, Confederate cavalry commanders Morgan and Forrest destroyed the railroads which immediately and significantly affected Buell's ability to remain in northern Alabama. Unable to supply his army with necessary food, fodder, and ammunition, Buell quickly altered his plans. He knew he must retreat to a manageable supply line.[18] In ordering Morgan to attack and sever Buell's supply line, Kirby Smith not only relieved pressure on

The railroad tunnels north of Gallatin, Tennessee.

the western edge of his department at Chattanooga, but also allowed Bragg to concoct an advance of his own into Tennessee and, ultimately, Kentucky.[19]

Alternate Scenario

Had Morgan been ordered to join Kirby Smith, the Rebel victory at Richmond, Kentucky, might have been even more one-sided. An additional reconnaissance force may have further assisted Kirby Smith. However, Morgan's successful damaging of the Louisville and Nashville Railroad was a spectacular logistical defeat for the Union.[20]

Nelson Splits His Forces between Richmond and Lancaster

Situation

Buell was aware of the movements of the various Confederate forces. With regard to his own situation, he sought reinforcements from General-in-Chief Henry Halleck and received two divisions from Grant's army. Once certain that Kirby Smith was moving into eastern Kentucky bypassing Cumberland Gap, Buell knew something had to be done to thwart him. Unless Brig. Gen. George Morgan's division protecting Cumberland Gap would pursue Kirby Smith, there were no troops available to challenge him. Buell would deduce that Kirby Smith's likely objective was Lexington or the capitol at Frankfort. Although Buell had enough problems watching Bragg and maintaining his supply while advancing on Chattanooga, he believed his responsibility encompassed the entire state of Kentucky. He was more than aware that he must somehow provide protection to the citizens of eastern Kentucky.[21]

Buell reacted to Kirby Smith's movements by sending some officers and men to Louisville to ascertain what was happening in and around the city, and to design some form of defense against Kirby Smith and his advancing army. This action would eliminate false rumors and provide a more precise evaluation of movements within the region. As a result, Buell could concentrate on deciphering Bragg's intentions. Therefore, on August 17, Buell ordered William "Bull" Nelson, a former navy lieutenant and current major general, to Kentucky with his division. Nelson took with him Brig. Gens. Mahlon Manson, Charles Cruft, and James S. Jackson.[22]

Because of Buell's concern for Bragg's pending movement, he wanted to concentrate on Bragg himself. To do so, Buell requested assistance that would allow him to remain in Tennessee while another force would confront Kirby Smith in eastern Kentucky. Where this other force might come from was questionable. Apparently without Buell's and Nelson's knowledge, Secretary

Maj. Gen. William "Bull" Nelson, USA.
Library of Congress.

of War Edwin Stanton had established the Military District of Kentucky, which lay within Buell's Department of the Ohio and fell under the Louisville command of Brig. Gen. Jeremiah Boyle. Boyle had been scrambling to put troops into the field to protect his area of command. Realizing the importance of defending Kentucky from invasion, on August 19, Stanton formed the new Military Department of the Ohio, which included Illinois, Indiana, Michigan, Ohio, Wisconsin, and that part of Kentucky east of the Tennessee River. Though Buell was unaware of them, these actions essentially constituted his Option 2. Stanton had appointed Maj. Gen. Horatio G. Wright to command this new department, with his headquarters located in Cincinnati. Thus Buell was relieved from command of the Department of the Ohio. However, he remained in command of his army and that part of Tennessee in which he was located.[23]

Wright arrived in Louisville on August 23 and assumed command of the new Department of the Ohio. Nelson arrived in Louisville that same day and was dumbfounded to learn of the new division and its commander. After he ascertained the new department's validity, Nelson received Wright's order to replace acting colonel and former major general Lew Wallace at Lexington, where he commanded the new Union Army of Kentucky. Nelson and his accompanying generals immediately complied with that order and arrived in Lexington on August 24. Wright ordered Nelson to defend Richmond,

Kentucky, if feasible. Otherwise, he was to fall back to a more defensible position such as the steep banks of the Kentucky River, north of Richmond. Unfortunately for the Union, Nelson chose to disperse his available troops somewhat differently.[24]

While Nelson understood the need to protect Richmond, around August 27 he became convinced that Kirby Smith's real objective was the Louisville and Nashville Railroad, located farther to the west. The Louisville and Nashville was Buell's major supply line, and he had ordered Nelson to help defend it. Even though Nelson no longer reported directly to Buell, he still would have wanted to support Buell in any way possible.[25]

Options

To best position his available troops, Nelson had four options. First, he could protect the Louisville and Nashville Railroad. Additionally, he could protect Richmond, or he could establish a defensive line at the Kentucky River. Nelson's last option was splitting his forces between these locations. Significantly affecting his choice of options was the lack of cavalry available to perform adequate reconnaissance of the advancing Rebel army.[26]

Option 1

Nelson was very concerned about his former commander Buell's request to protect his (Buell's) railroad supply line from Louisville to Nashville. Instinctively, Nelson deemed this a proper course of action; he could maneuver his available force to block Kirby Smith's advance toward the line. This choice would help protect the railroad, but it would open up other avenues of advance—such as to Richmond, Kentucky—for Kirby Smith and his small army.[27]

Option 2

Nelson had to be concerned that Kirby Smith might march directly toward Richmond, Kentucky, and that the city was an objective of his advance. If Kirby Smith's Rebels captured Richmond, the way was open to Lexington and Frankfort, Kentucky's capital. Stopping Kirby Smith at Richmond would put an end to the heretofore successful Confederate advance. However, the city offered little in the way of physical barriers or substantial defensive terrain, thus providing little assistance to the Yankees attempting to protect it.[28]

Option 3

Far and away the best defensive position to confront the Rebel army advancing on Richmond was the Kentucky River. North of Richmond, the river was lined with steep, easily defendable banks, providing a strong barrier to Kirby Smith's army as it attempted to advance north toward Lexington and Frankfort. However, defending the Kentucky River position would allow the Rebels to handily capture Richmond, although the town itself might be of little value within the big picture.[29]

Option 4

If Nelson split his forces, he might better prepare to intercept Kirby Smith's army no matter which objective he chose. Assigning troops to Richmond, the Kentucky River, or Lancaster/Danville (to protect the railroad) would give Nelson this advantage. However, in dividing his troops, he would have fewer defenders present unless he had time to shift troops as Kirby Smith's destination became clearer.[30]

Decision

Nelson made the critical decision to defend the railroad as Buell had desired. In expectation of Kirby Smith's advance, Nelson ordered the Third Brigade of the Army of Kentucky to Danville and a newly formed brigade to Lancaster. This action split his command roughly in half, with two brigades under the overall authority of Brig. Gen. Mahlon Manson remaining at Richmond.[31]

Results/Impact

By splitting his command, Nelson seriously weakened his force under Manson that was to defend Richmond. This decision left Manson with some seven thousand men, the vast majority of whom were brand-new enlistees, untrained in the art of warfare. Nelson was unaware that his command under Manson would soon face two divisions of veteran soldiers led by Kirby Smith. Though of equal numbers to Manson's troops, Kirby Smith's men were possessed of far superior fighting ability. While Nelson made an understandable decision in light of his assumption about where Kirby Smith would attack, splitting the Union force led to defeat at Richmond, the loss of much territory including Richmond and Lexington, and casualties in significant numbers.[32]

Alternate Scenario

Had Nelson kept his entire command intact at Richmond, their sheer numbers might have repulsed Kirby Smith. However, Kirby Smith did have two brigades of Heth's Division a day's march to his rear, and he could have postponed his attack until Heth was up and in the line of battle.[33]

Kirby Smith Decides to Attack the Union Force at Richmond

Situation

As Kirby Smith advanced farther into Kentucky, he had one major concern: Where would he encounter Union opposition? Logically, the Union command would find a location that could easily be defended, entrench, and provide a serious obstacle to Confederate advance. Aware of the terrain, Kirby Smith feared that the Union force sent to block his advance would utilize the idea of former major general Lew Wallace. North of Richmond, the Kentucky River's superior, naturally vertical riverbanks provided an excellent line of defense for the Union. Brief small combats at Mount Vernon and Big Hill did not affect Kirby Smith's advance into the Bluegrass region of Kentucky.[34]

Options

Smith had three options: continue his advance on Lexington, attempt to rejoin Bragg, or change his objective to another location.[35]

Option 1

Kirby Smith was marching unimpeded into Kentucky. Until challenged by a Federal defensive force, and as long as he could supply his men appropriately, Kirby Smith could easily continue toward Lexington. Moving farther north, he continued to believe in his role as savior of Kentucky. As time passed, he could continue to rely on his cavalry for reconnaissance. Upon the discovery of a Federal force preparing to block his advance, particularly at the Kentucky River, Kirby Smith could reconsider his objective. He was already near Richmond, Kentucky, located about twenty-seven miles south of Lexington.[36]

Option 2

With the axiom "There is strength in numbers," Kirby Smith could shift his objective to reuniting with Bragg. Under the general's protection, Kirby Smith would be largely free from fear of assault on his small army alone. Joining with Bragg would divert the junior officer's advance, but more importantly, it would place him under Bragg's command. This arrangement did not appeal to Kirby Smith's independent nature.[37]

Option 3

Kirby Smith could alter his objective and march toward another, less defended one. As he advanced farther into the interior of Kentucky, he could reexamine what his true goal should be.[38]

Decision

Upon learning that the Rebel force assigned to protect Lexington was entrenching south of the city at Richmond, Kentucky, rather than along the north banks of the Kentucky River, Kirby Smith made the critical decision to continue to advance on Richmond. He had full confidence in his two lead divisions, commanded by veteran officers with combat experience, and in his nearly six thousand combat-hardened troops. Kirby Smith also felt that the odds favored his attack; his men would most likely perform well against the raw Union soldiers they faced.[39]

Results/Impact

On August 28, Kirby Smith surmised that the Union command at Richmond was going to give him battle south of that city. The next day, Col. John Scott's cavalrymen encountered Union troops south of Richmond that not only rebuffed them but pursued them back to Kirby Smith's main force. This confrontation confirmed his decision to attack, as he now realized the Union command would not be well entrenched behind the Kentucky River.[40]

Alternate Scenario

From the perspective of the Union force sent to resist Kirby Smith's advancing army, the northern banks of the Kentucky River provided a much more favorable defensive position. Had Nelson ordered his various troops to dig in there, Kirby Smith undoubtedly would not have ordered an assault on this almost impregnable position. Kirby Smith would have been forced to bypass this target or find another one for his army to acquire. As a result, the Battle of Richmond would not have taken place. The Union would not have lost over four thousand soldiers, and Kirby Smith would not likely have captured Lexington. In retrospect it is hard to understand why Nelson and the Union were not quick to take advantage of this natural defensive terrain.[41]

Bragg Invades Kentucky, Bypassing Nashville

Situation

Also on August 28, Bragg began his movement out of Chattanooga. Kirby Smith's violation of their mutual agreement to eventually join forces after the capture of Cumberland Gap forced Bragg to reevaluate his future plans. Nevertheless, Bragg still was in position to engineer a movement to confound the Union forces in Tennessee and Kentucky. Having some five different pathways out of Chattanooga, he could initially confuse the Federals as to his intended destination. Bragg had come to Chattanooga with some thirty-six thousand men. After giving Kirby Smith McCown's and Cleburne's Divisions, he had about twenty-seven thousand men of all arms as he prepared to advance.[42]

Options

Bragg now had three options: He could attempt to recapture Nashville, the capital of Tennessee. He could advance into Kentucky to join up with Kirby Smith's small army and maneuver to hold that state for the Confederacy. The last possibility was for Bragg to temporarily disregard Kirby Smith, remain in East Tennessee, protect the all-important rail hub at Chattanooga, and perhaps force Buell to do battle somewhere other than Nashville.[43]

Option 1

Both sides logically anticipated that Bragg and the Confederacy would wish to recapture Nashville for political and resource reasons. Freeing Middle Tennessee of Federal control would have tremendous psychological advantages for the South, and allow it to benefit from the many resources within the region. Many, including Confederate governor of Tennessee Isham Harris, urged Bragg to retake Nashville. Bragg, however, believed the city might be defended by such a large force that his own army, by itself, would not be sufficiently strong to capture it. Even if his troops did so, he believed the casualties would be too costly.[44]

Option 2

Bragg could temporarily ignore Nashville and advance into Kentucky. This option would force Buell and the Federal command to protect Louisville and attempt to challenge Bragg. The enlistment of thousands of Kentuckian men in the Rebel military would be vital to Bragg's plans for holding the state. Combining his army with Kirby Smith's would give Bragg a substantial force with which to counter Union attacks. Effectively capturing Kentucky for the Confederacy would have tremendous positive political and geographical consequences in terms of additional resources for the region. It made sense to Bragg to invade Kentucky, join forces with Kirby Smith, defeat the Union in battle there, and capture Kentucky for the Confederacy. As did Kirby Smith, Bragg assumed that huge numbers of Kentuckians were chafing under Union control and simply waiting for the Confederacy to liberate them. Thousands of men would quickly join his army, increasing his ability to capture and hold on to the commonwealth.[45]

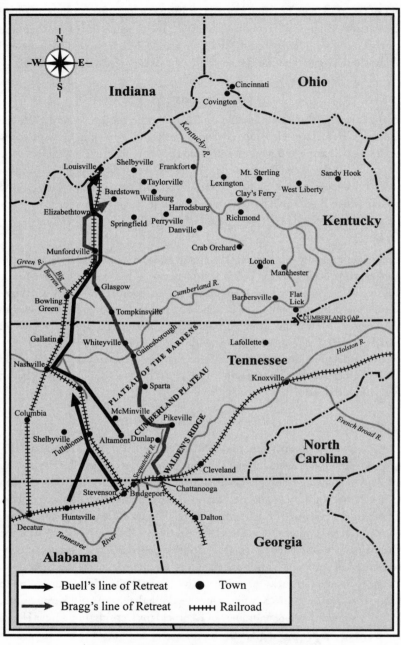

Route of Bragg's Invasion of Kentucky,
August 26 to October 8, 1862

Option 3

Bragg could position his army such that it would protect Chattanooga and its railroad hub, while potentially luring Buell to fight outside of Nashville. This option would leave Kirby Smith on his own in Kentucky, but would not give away possession of Chattanooga. The downside to this option was that he would be independently dealing with Federals in Kentucky who would very likely outnumber him.[46]

Decision

Having decided on this advance, Bragg intended to capture Louisville. As Buell and other Union officers began to sense this objective, panic quickly arose in Louisville and even Cincinnati, as it appeared that Bragg could arrive at Louisville ahead of Buell and other Union reinforcements.[47]

Results/Impact

When he decided on this movement, Bragg quickly placed the Confederates on the offense. The Union high command assumed the defense, with Buell now in a race to Bragg's assumed target: Louisville. This would eventually force Bragg to make further critical decisions as he marched into Kentucky. As he began his march he believed, as Kirby Smith had informed him, that thousands of Kentucky men would quickly join his army, strengthening his ability to capture and retain that state. Bragg stated that he had some "15,000 stand of arms and no one to use them." This incorrect assumption would prove a disappointment.[48]

Alternate Scenario

Bragg would probably have failed had he attempted to recapture Nashville; the effort would have entailed attacking a larger Federal army entrenched around the city. More importantly, failing at Nashville would have reduced Bragg's chances of even beginning what became the Kentucky Campaign of 1862, certainly providing a different outcome that summer. Exactly what that outcome would have been is subject for the reader's conjecture.[49]

CHAPTER 3

THE BATTLE OF RICHMOND, KENTUCKY, AUGUST 30, 1862

As the Battle of Richmond was about to begin, three critical decisions, one by the initial Union commander and two by the Confederate commander, led to the raw Federal troops' decisive defeat. This battle is often unnoticed in Civil War lore, yet it was the most lopsided victory of that conflict, and a boon to Confederate morale.

Manson Moves South of Richmond to Defend the City

Situation

Brig. Gen. Mahlon Manson, now in command of the Federal Army of Kentucky forces near Richmond, was acutely aware of Kirby Smith's advance toward that city. Once in the area, Manson recognized that he must take some kind of action to stymie Kirby Smith's continued progress into the Bluegrass region. Virtually all of the Union commander's soldiers were brand-new to military service, a fact that left him gravely concerned. Many, if not most, of the men could neither load nor fire their weapons. Therefore, if Manson was to confront Kirby Smith, he needed to do more than determine a location for doing so. To command his fresh levies in battle with any hope of success, Manson had to continuously instruct them in handling firearms and conduct drills for them at all levels.[1]

Options

As the on scene commander, Manson had three options available to him. He could establish a defensive line on the north side of the Kentucky River, or he could advance to meet Kirby Smith's army somewhere south of the river. A final option involved Manson's retreating to another suitable position closer to reinforcements, thus sacrificing Richmond for the present.[2]

Option 1

The best defensive position in the area was the Kentucky River's high, steep north banks. Even raw troops would see the advantage of this location and be more likely to remain and defend it. Likewise, Kirby Smith would be too smart to risk losing part of his army in assaulting that position. However, establishing this defensive line would surrender Richmond to Kirby Smith.[3]

Option 2

Manson could protect both Lexington and Richmond by marching to a defensible location south of Richmond and preparing to resist Kirby Smith's advancing army. It was unknown exactly where Manson and his men could station themselves. This option would violate Nelson's orders to establish a defensive position on the north bank of the Kentucky River (although Manson would claim not to have received that order until after the fighting had begun). Manson reasoned that it might be more appropriate to attempt to protect Richmond than to retreat through the city, forfeiting it to the Confederates. However, immediately south of Richmond, the terrain was less suitable than the north bank of the Kentucky River for providing its defenders with any significant protection.[4]

Option 3

With raw troops, many not even knowledgeable enough to fire their weapons, retreating to a better defensible position would allow Manson conserve his manpower while seeking additional reinforcements. The location of this defensible position remains somewhat doubtful. Also, withdrawal to this site would cede a considerable amount of territory to Kirby Smith.[5]

Decision

On October 29, Manson made the critical decision to move out and establish a defensive line south of Richmond. His precise location was approximately a mile south of Rogersville, a little north of Kingston, and just south of the Mount Zion Church. Placing his men on both sides of the Richmond Road and perpendicular to it, he made his final troop dispositions. He then prepared for the arrival of Kirby Smith's Confederates. Unaware of Nelson's order to retreat and not give battle (supposedly, Manson didn't receive this order until after the battle had begun), Manson gambled that his raw troops would be able to hold off the enemy. In addition, he apparently did not realize the strength of Kirby Smith's divisions. Kirby Smith's battle-hardened officers and men were some of the better regiments within the Confederacy. The result of Manson's decision to fight south of Richmond would soon have huge ramifications for the Union cause in Kentucky.[6]

Results/Impact

Manson's critical decision played right into the hands of Kirby Smith, who had feared the Federals would retreat to the Kentucky River rather than fight. The Confederate officer prepared his men for battle as soon as he realized the Union's intentions. Kirby Smith remained confident that his battle-tested veterans were as fine an army as any, and he had faith in their ability to win this contest. Manson's movement south of Richmond resulted in the Battle of Richmond, Kentucky.[7]

Alternate Scenarios

Either of the other options available to Manson would likely have resulted in a better outcome for the Federals. In hindsight, pitting untested, largely untrained and untested men against hardened combat veterans was obviously a mistake. Temporarily abandoning Richmond, which was lost anyway, would have been less costly to the Union cause. Establishing a defensive line on the north bank of the Kentucky River north of Richmond would have given Manson's raw troops a psychological advantage. The then-entrenched Yankees would also have been much more likely to hold this natural defensive location. Likewise, a retreat back to another more defensible site would have increased the Union's odds of success.[8]

Kirby Smith Orders Flank Attacks against Manson

Situation

Late on the twenty-ninth, Manson sent Union cavalry to slow Kirby Smith's approach, but these soldiers had little effect. Early on the thirtieth, Manson ordered his troops to man a ridge just south of the Mount Zion Church astride the Richmond Road, on a low ridge running perpendicular to it. As Kirby Smith's army advanced up the Richmond Road toward that town, it

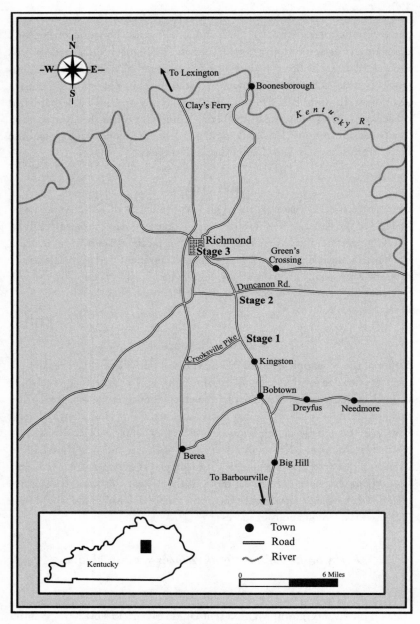

Three Phases of the Battle of Richmond, Kentucky,
August 30, 1862

began to receive artillery fire from a Union battery commanded by Lieut. Edwin O. Lamphere.[9]

As Kirby Smith marched into the looming battle, two of his divisions took the field—Brig. Gen. Thomas J. Churchill's and Brig. Gen. Patrick Cleburne's. (For the most part, Brig. Gen. Carter L. Stevenson's division was still guarding Cumberland Gap, while Brig. Gen. Henry Heth's division was some distance to the rear but also advancing.) Col. John Scott's cavalry brigade was also available to Kirby Smith. The Confederate officer was a hero of the Battle of Bull Run or Manassas and a combat veteran. Churchill, Cleburne, and their men were also combat veterans, so Kirby Smith felt that Manson's force would be no match against his own.[10] As the battle began, Kirby Smith wanted to deploy his army in a manner that utilized its experience, confounded the enemy, and maximized the chances of victory. While confident in his soldiers' ability, he had no desire to sacrifice them in meaningless attacks. Thus Kirby Smith and his subordinate commanders would weigh their options carefully.[11]

Options

Four options would allow Kirby Smith to maximize his likelihood of success while minimizing his potential casualties. He could directly assault the Union position with the belief that it would quickly fold up. Alternatively, he could attempt to flank either the Union left or the Union right. Finally, Kirby Smith could try to outflank both the Union left and right flanks.[12]

Option 1

Arguably the riskier option in terms of casualties, a direct assault by Kirby Smith's combat-hardened veterans on Manson's raw, largely untrained soldiers could reasonably and quickly be successful. The Confederate commander would consider the likelihood of the Union soldiers only firing a few rounds at best before being overrun. However, a direct assault would cost at least some casualties.[13]

Option 2

A creek named Mound Branch, located just south of the Mount Zion Church and flowing north to south, had created a small ravine paralleling the Richmond Road about a quarter mile to its west. This would provide a hidden access to a point very near Manson's right flank, positioned west of the Richmond Road and the Armstrong House. A Rebel brigade or two could utilize this approach to advance on the Federals and arrive undetected, resulting in few if any casualties until the Confederates were almost on top of soldiers from the Sixty-Ninth Indiana. Manson had positioned these troops to protect his right flank.[14]

Option 3

Although not as well-protected as the site described in Option 2, some ravines and woods near the Union left flank would likely provide the Rebels access to that portion of the enemy troops, defended by parts of two Indiana regiments, the 69th and 116th. A Confederate flanking force could potentially roll up the Union left flank. The possibility of fewer casualties and the effect of surprising the Federal soldiers would make this a good choice.[15]

Option 4

A final option would be for Kirby Smith to utilize Options 2 and 3 and attempt to outmaneuver both Union flanks. This course of action would force the Union troops to defend both flanks and not allow troops from one flank to move to the assistance of the other.[16]

Decision

Kirby Smith made the critical decision to utilize Option 4 and assault both of Manson's flanks instead of his center.[17]

Results/Impact

During the Civil War, flank attacks were one of the most effective means of defeating the enemy. Armies usually fought in lines of battle where their firepower was most effective. It followed that the flanks were vulnerable to assaults, although they could be "refused" or bent back to provide some linear firepower for defense. Usually, soldiers who discovered the enemy rolling up their flank(s) retreated quickly.[18]

Kirby Smith initiated flanking attacks on Manson's right and left while maintaining direct fire at his line in order to disguise these movements. He ordered Col. Thomas H. McCray's brigade of Churchill's Division, preceded by Clark's Arkansas Sharpshooters, to advance up Mound Branch and assault Manson's right flank. Kirby Smith also directed Cleburne to send a force out to assault Manson's left flank. Cleburne ordered Acting Brig. Gen. Preston Smith to send a regiment toward the Union left, and Smith promptly dispatched the 154th Tennessee on that advance. Shortly before being wounded in his mouth, Cleburne ordered Preston Smith to advance his three remaining regiments to the Union left as well. Both of these flanking maneuvers were successful, and the Union line quickly collapsed. The raw, broken

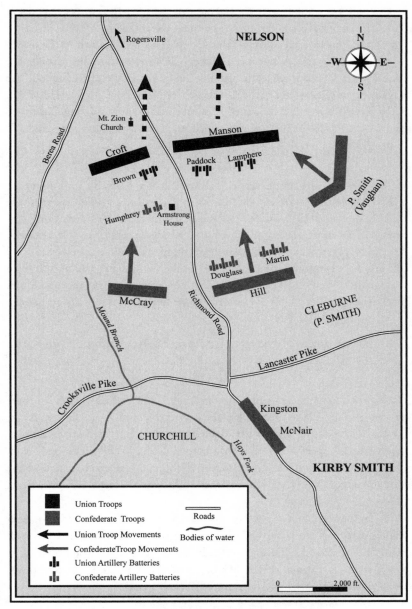

First Phase, Battle of Richmond, Kentucky, August 30, 1862

Federal units streamed north for the moment with Kirby Smith's veterans in pursuit. This initial rout of Manson's command was the first of three phases of fighting that portended the one-sided Confederate victory later in the day.[19]

From the Confederacy's perspective, Cleburne's wounding during the flanking attacks was perhaps the greatest loss of the Battle of Richmond. The brigadier general was shot in the mouth, rendering him literally speechless. Yet Kirby Smith's command continued its successful advance, utilizing Cleburne's tactics with Preston Smith assuming Cleburne's role as division commander.[20]

Alternate Scenario

With veterans of the Battles of Belmont and Shiloh, Kirby Smith would have had had little to fear from a direct assault against raw Federal recruits. He could have massed his men and ordered a charge instead of the flanking maneuvers. This effort would undoubtedly have been successful as well, although the casualty list would likely have been higher. Untrained, newly enlisted Union soldiers would not have had the discipline to repulse an assault from seasoned Rebels with fixed bayonets. The charge would have resulted in the quick folding of the Union line, a similar outcome to what actually occurred.[21]

Kirby Smith Prepares to Capture Fleeing Union Troops

Situation

Unbeknown to its participants, the Battle of Richmond was fought in three separate phases. Phase One took place near the Mount Zion Church, flanking both sides of the Richmond Road. Phase Two unfolded at the Duncanon Road and Speedwell Road, both perpendicular to the Richmond Road. Phase Three occurred largely within the Richmond Cemetery located on the southern edge of town. All three phases of the battle resulted in Confederate victories.[22]

After routing Manson's command near the Mount Zion Church, Manson managed to re-form it farther north along the Duncanon and Speedwell Roads intersecting the Richmond Road. Phase Two of the battle would occur at this location. Even at this early juncture of the fighting, Kirby Smith was already planning ahead and debating several options.[23]

Options

Kirby Smith had three choices for utilizing his cavalry during the battle: Firstly, he could order Scott to provide additional reconnaissance. Another option involved maneuvering north of Richmond in anticipation of capturing

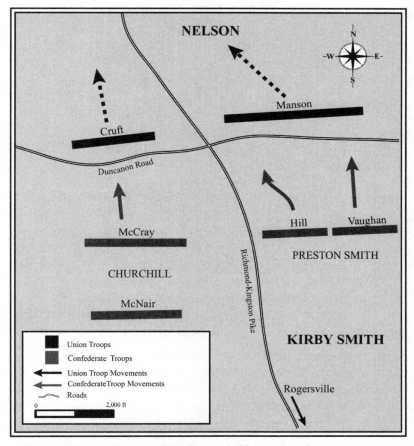

Second Phase, Battle of Richmond, Kentucky, August 30, 1862

routed Federal soldiers there. As a last alternative, Kirby Smith could order Scott to attack one of the Union flanks during the battle.[24]

Option 1

Kirby Smith could utilize his cavalry under Col. John Scott to provide reconnaissance as the battle unfolded. In its traditional role as Kirby Smith's eyes and ears, the cavalry would provide up-to-date information on other Federal troops in the area, as well as validate current Union maneuvering. However, Kirby Smith already was well apprised as to the enemy's positions.[25]

Col. John S. Scott, CSA. From *Howell Carter,*
A Cavalryman's Reminiscences of the Civil War.

Option 2

Another option was to send Col. John Scott's cavalry north of Richmond via a route west of the Richmond Road in expectation of routing the raw Union troops. Using Scott's cavalry, Kirby Smith could set a trap to capture Yankees attempting to escape north of Richmond while they were on their way to the Kentucky River and eventually Lexington.[26]

Option 3

Kirby Smith could utilize his cavalry as a flanking force, as it could quickly advance and attack the Union left or right at any stage of the battle. This option would provide a disruptive force exactly where the Federal command did not need one. However, it would also eliminate Scott from providing reconnaissance or other duties as assigned.[27]

Decision

Kirby Smith made the critical decision to order Colonel Scott to leave the scene of the fighting and maneuver north of Richmond. The Confederate commander anticipated a victory so successful that retreating Yankees would flee through Richmond and be susceptible to capture north of that town.[28]

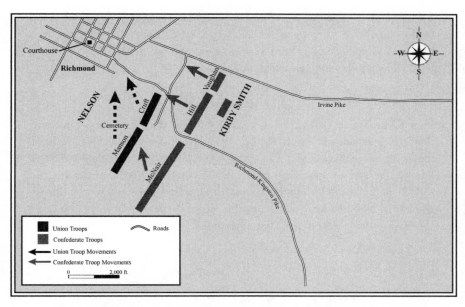

Third Phase, Battle of Richmond, Kentucky, August 30, 1862

Results/Impact

Kirby Smith's choice proved to be very astute, as the battle unfolded into a Rebel rout of the Yankees at all three phases. Kirby Smith's confidence in his command allowed for the positioning of Scott in advance of the Union retreat and rout after the fighting concluded at Phase Three.[29]

At 2:30 a.m. in Lexington, Maj. Gen. William "Bull" Nelson finally received notification of Manson's defensive position south of Richmond. Nelson rode to the battlefield and arrived in time to encourage his men before their final attempt at halting the Rebel advance at the Richmond Cemetery. His Yankees were quickly overrun despite his vigorous attempts to have them hold their position, and the retreat/rout began.[30]

Meanwhile, Colonel Scott had aligned his cavalry force north along the Lexington Pike leading from Richmond to Lexington, the most plausible escape route for Yankees evading capture. Exactly as Kirby Smith had gambled, the surviving Federal soldiers commenced retreating as fast as they could. While some paused in Richmond to rest and regroup, most continued on, following the Lexington Pike. While the day grew dark and some escaped,

Scott and his men rounded up thousands of these Yankees and escorted them to the courthouse area for safekeeping. In all, Scott's cavalry captured over four thousand Federal prisoners, adding immensely to the Rebel victory. Kirby Smith's decision paid off most handsomely.[31]

Alternate Scenario

Had Kirby Smith utilized Scott's cavalry to either charge the Union line directly or assault one of its flanks, this additional manpower would have increased his chances of victory. At the same time, many more defeated Yankees would have escaped. This consequence would have reduced the magnitude of Kirby Smith's victory and cost him a least a few more men in direct combat with the Federal soldiers in the line of battle, not those running for their lives, often without carrying a weapon.[32]

CHAPTER 4

THE KENTUCKY CAMPAIGN CONTINUES, AUGUST 31–OCTOBER 7, 1862

While events leading up to the Battle of Richmond, Kentucky, took place in eastern and central Kentucky, both armies under Buell and Bragg were also maneuvering. Seven critical decisions prior to the decisive Battle of Perryville, Kentucky, directly caused the fighting. Both commanders made choices and reacted to others as they thought best for their side.

Buell Decides to Retreat to Nashville

Situation

Maj. Gen. Don Carlos Buell had been unsuccessful in following his orders to advance from Corinth to capture Chattanooga. Because of the lack of supplies and forage, as well as the intense drought, he had no interest in advancing into eastern Kentucky or eastern Tennessee. President Abraham Lincoln wanted Federal intervention into eastern Tennessee because of Union loyalists residing there.[1]

As previously noted, Gen. Braxton Bragg had initially agreed to deploy Maj. Gen. John P. McCown's division to Chattanooga to provide Kirby Smith reinforcements he desperately believed he needed on June 26. Bragg did so partly to get rid of McCown, whom he despised, and partly to see whether travel by railroad was logical in this situation. McCown and his men traveled some 776 miles on six separate railroads and a ferry ride across Mobile Bay, arriving in Chattanooga on July 3, a spectacular transportation feat for the Confederacy. Bragg followed up McCown's successful travels with the rest of his army less the wagons and artillery, which went overland south of the Memphis and Charleston Railroad. The first units arrived on July 27, but it took two more weeks for the rest of his men to make the journey. In stark contrast, it took Bragg's wagons and artillery six long weeks to travel a much shorter distance to Chattanooga. Meanwhile, Bragg and Kirby Smith met and agreed to cooperate as described in a critical decision above. As Bragg and his army left Chattanooga, what action should Buell undertake to confront them?[2]

Options

Buell's three options were as follows: moving to attack Bragg as he advanced out of Chattanooga, retreating to Nashville in order to protect it, or advancing into Kentucky to defend the Bowling Green line and eventually repel Bragg.[3]

Option 1

Buell had the option of confronting Bragg's army as it left Chattanooga on August 28. If he successfully attacked the smaller enemy force before it had marched very far, he could prevent Bragg from recapturing Nashville and advancing into Kentucky. The Lincoln administration would undoubtedly favor this kind of action. However, Buell would have to quickly reassemble his army, call for reinforcements, discern Bragg's destination, track him down, and give battle, perhaps not at a place of his choosing.[4]

Option 2

Buell could order his various units to march immediately to Nashville in order to protect that city. With his army entrenched around Nashville, Bragg would be at a disadvantage in attempting to assault Buell there. Buell had made known his distaste for maneuvering in eastern Tennessee, and this option was appealing.[5]

Option 3

If Bragg was planning an invasion of Kentucky, it was Buell's responsibility to counteract that movement, and he needed to do so before Bragg made any significant headway into this controversial commonwealth that both sides claimed. A confrontation with the Rebels would permit Buell to protect Kentucky and drive Bragg out of it altogether.[6]

Decision

Buell made the critical decision to retreat toward Nashville. On August 26, elements of Bragg's army were spotted crossing the Tennessee River at Bridgeport. Therefore, deciding not to aggressively move on Bragg, Buell ordered a retreat to Murfreesboro, where his supplies were concentrated. He would gather his army here while closely observing Bragg's advance.[7]

Results/Impact

By retreating toward Nashville, Buell gave Bragg the advantage of maneuver and forced himself to react to Bragg's choice of movements. Buell did not know that the Confederate commander himself was continuously changing his mind as to his objective. Bragg had been given an opportunity to steal the lead on Buell, and he now had the ability to do exactly that. However, both leaders were troubled with politics and feeding their armies while on the move. Both men were pushed to accomplish great things; it remained to be seen whether they would. At this time Buell had the opportunity to aggressively maneuver to assault Bragg. He gave up this chance in order to protect his supply depot at Nashville. This may be explained by his military training, strongly influenced by the military theorist Antoine H. Jomini, who advocated holding territory versus destroying enemy armies.[8]

Alternate Scenario

Had Buell been an aggressive commander, he could have consolidated his various units at Sparta or another location near Bragg's potential line of march and prepared to challenge him. An early victory over Bragg would have radically changed the Kentucky Campaign as we know it today. With Bragg kept from entering Kentucky or even Nashville, Kirby Smith would have been largely on his own and subject to Union forces raised along the Ohio River. He would probably have been forced to retreat much sooner than he (and Bragg) actually did.[9]

Bragg Orders the Capture of the Garrison at Munfordville

Situation

Buell finally realized that, instead of attempting to recover Nashville for the Confederacy, Bragg was moving north and threatening such cities as Louisville and Cincinnati. Therefore, Buell hastened north, arriving in Bowling Green, Kentucky, on September 14 at the same time that Bragg reached

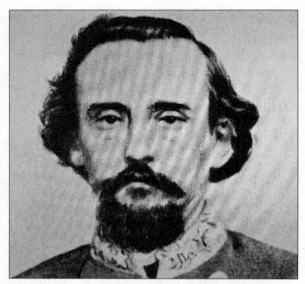

Brig. Gen. James R. Chalmers, CSA. *The Photographic History of the Civil War, Vol. IV.*

Glasgow, thirty-three miles east. With Kirby Smith's decision to move into Kentucky on his own, Bragg was forced to keep his army between Buell's and Kirby Smith's. Otherwise, at least theoretically, Buell could go after and destroy Kirby Smith's small force, then attack Bragg, who would be unsupported.[10]

Bragg ordered a small advance force consisting of Brig. Gen. James R. Chalmers's brigade to move farther north to Cave City, where it arrived on September 12. From here an interesting event took place. Kirby Smith had ordered cavalry commander Col. John Scott (of Battle of Richmond fame) and a brigade of three hundred cavalrymen to observe Bragg's location while also destroying bridges on the Louisville and Nashville Railroad. The most important of these bridges was at Munfordville; it had a span of 1,800 feet and stood some 115 feet above the Green River. When Scott and his men arrived at Munfordville, he demanded the surrender of the 1,800-member Union camp protecting the bridge. The Federals quickly refused to do so. Therefore, Scott sent a messenger to Chalmers informing him that the Rebel cavalry would attack the following morning and asking whether Chalmers desired to join in the assault.[11]

Like so many commanders in the war, Chalmers was interested in obtaining new glory and promotion, and so he seized on this opportunity. Without informing Bragg of his intentions, he launched the offensive at 5 a.m. on the fourteenth. After four and a half hours of unsuccessful attacks and the failure of Union commander Col. John Wilder to surrender, Chalmers retreated to Cave City. When Bragg learned of Chalmers's "unauthorized and injudicious" repulse, he was angered. What should he do concerning this situation? [12]

Options

Bragg had three options: he could bypass Munfordville completely and continue marching toward Kirby Smith; he could send additional troops to attack and capture the Federal garrison there; or he could detour his entire army there to ensure the capture of the garrison.[13]

Option 1

Although a tempting target, the railroad bridge at Munfordville was one of many, and the Louisville and Nashville Railroad had already been seriously constrained by Forrest's and Morgan's raids. Was incurring the delay in advancing farther into Kentucky worth it? Yet the loss of this bridge to the Union supply line would obviously benefit the Rebel cause.[14]

Railroad bridge near Munfordville, across the Green River. *Harper's Weekly.*

Option 2

While Chalmers's brigade had lost almost three hundred men, dispatching a sufficiently larger force to Munfordville could easily overrun Wilder's garrison while incurring a reasonable number of casualties. Any embarrassment resulting from Chalmers's unauthorized attack would be erased, and Bragg's army could be quickly on the move again.[15]

Option 3

Bragg's final option was to march his entire army to Munfordville to ensure the capture of the Union garrison stationed there. This option would make up for the black eye on the Army of the Mississippi that Wilder's defeat of Chalmers had caused. However, marching to Munfordville would definitely delay Bragg's advance into Kentucky, and it would potentially allow Buell time to maneuver.[16]

Decision

Bragg chose to march his entire army to Munfordville and capture the garrison there.[17]

Results/Impact

Bragg's army advanced on the afternoon of September 15, traveling some thirty-five miles and arriving at Munfordville early on the sixteenth after a tough night march. After establishing a fortified ring around the Union garrison, Bragg demanded its surrender. The new Union commander, Col. Cyrus Dunham, whose Fiftieth Indiana had marched to Munfordville to reinforce Wilder, requested direction from Union headquarters at Louisville. The response was to place Wilder, whom Dunham had superseded, back in command! Trying to stall for time, Wilder requested a suspension of hostilities. In one of the more bizarre events of the war, he agreed to surrender if Bragg could prove that he indeed had the superior manpower. After a tour of the Rebel ranks and cannon surrounding him, Wilder capitulated. Bragg gained four thousand Yankee prisoners and small arms at no additional cost to his army—a welcome victory.[18]

However, Buell took advantage of Bragg's delay at Munfordville, continuing to advance instead of halting at Bowling Green. Bragg concentrated his force at Munfordville and awaited Buell's attack there. That strike never transpired. After vacillating more, Bragg finally ordered his army to march to Bardstown. Although some historians argue that Munfordville would have been a great place for Bragg to do battle with Buell, what is often overlooked is the fact that this region had already been foraged over, and it lacked available water. This circumstance allowed Buell to march directly to Louisville, where he could refit and resupply his ragged men. The capture of Munfordville changed the campaign, as it allowed Buell to retreat to Louisville.[19]

Alternate Scenario

Had Bragg been a more aggressive commander, he could have ignored the situation at Munfordville and moved to block Buell's retreat to Louisville. This might have forced Buell to attack Bragg, giving Bragg better odds. If Bragg were able to damage Buell here, it would have disrupted the Union presence in Kentucky, to the advantage of the Confederacy. However, Bragg could have been outflanked by Buell and moved into Bragg's rear, compromising his ability to join with Kirby Smith, as described next.[20]

Bragg Decides Not to Fight Buell but to Join Kirby Smith

Situation

After the events at Munfordville, Bragg expected Buell to attack him there. Bragg had outmarched Buell to the city, but Buell had quickly marched from Glasgow toward Cave City. However, Buell's ardor cooled considerably when he viewed the results of the fighting at Munfordville. He learned from Wilder that Bragg's army was preparing significant defenses at Munfordville and that Kirby Smith's army was to join him there. Meanwhile, Bragg was indeed ready to give battle to Buell, but Buell would be on the offense and Bragg on the defense.[21]

Options

At this time Bragg had five options: First, he could remain on the defense at Munfordville and await an attack by Buell. Alternatively, he could try and order Kirby Smith to join him in the upcoming battle, if there was to be one, or he could decide to abandon Munfordville and join with Kirby Smith at Bardstown. Another option would be going on the offense and attacking Buell, possibly near Elizabethtown, perhaps augmented with Kirby Smith. Lastly, Bragg could march back to Nashville and retake that less heavily defended city.[22]

Option 1

Entrenched around Munfordville, where the odds favored him, Bragg was comfortable in allowing Buell to attack him there. Would Buell suddenly become aggressive? However, in spite of many predictions, remaining there any length of time was problematic as little food could be had in the area, which Yankees had already visited during earlier maneuvering.[23]

Option 2

Bragg could increase the odds of success in a battle at Munfordville if he could get Kirby Smith to join him there. Kirby Smith had so far indicated no propensity to place himself under Bragg's command; he enjoyed independent authority too much. If he did consent to march to Munfordville and serve under Bragg, the odds would definitely favor Bragg were he attacked.[24]

Option 3

Retreating from Munfordville would solve the provisions problem, and joining Kirby Smith at Bardstown would augment Bragg's army and allow him to dictate a coordinated effort against Buell. Would Kirby Smith cooperate with Bragg? [25]

Option 4

If Buell was not going to attack Bragg at Munfordville, he would likely hasten to Louisville to refit and resupply his men. If Bragg could cut Buell off and challenge him in battle, perhaps near Elizabethtown or prior to reaching Louisville, he could render Buell ineffective. With Kirby Smith reinforcing him, Bragg would have a significant edge in such a battle. However, Kirby Smith would have to agree to join and also march quickly to make this happen.[26]

Option 5

A final option would be for Bragg to exit Kentucky and advance on Nashville. This Rebel capital was not as well defended as some, and recapturing it would gain Bragg political capital as well. Of course, this course of action would leave Kentucky to the Union and also leave Kirby Smith to operate on his own.[27]

Decision

Bragg made the critical decision to abandon a battle with Buell at this time and join Kirby Smith's army in Bardstown. With the two armies united, Bragg would be able, for the moment, to challenge Buell's army. Defeating Buell might well give Kentucky over to the Confederacy.[28]

Results/Impact

By deciding to march to Bardstown, Bragg gave Buell a free direct path to Louisville, where his headquarters and supplies were located. The citizens of Louisville and its surrounding communities feared Bragg's pillaging, and they went to extremes to construct fortifications in these locations, especially Louisville. Thousands of troops were sent to the city to defend it.[29]

Buell took advantage of Bragg's not challenging his retreat to Louisville, and his impoverished Federals began to straggle into that city on September 25. Over the next few days the remainder of Buell's exhausted army arrived there to safety. Buell commenced resting, refitting, and resupplying his army.[30]

Ignoring Buell gave him a second chance to move against Bragg and Kirby Smith, and this opportunity would culminate in the Battle of Perryville. Bragg's critical decision essentially gave up the offensive, effectively setting up the demise of the Kentucky Campaign of 1862 for the Confederacy. Yet Bragg determined that he could not leave Kirby Smith to fend off a probable movement and attempt at destruction by the Union command of his small army.[31]

Alternate Scenario

Had Bragg taken the offense and attacked Buell, he might well have effectively stopped Buell's army from further harming the Confederacy. The Union high command would have eventually regrouped and raised another army. However, that process would have taken time, and Northern morale would have suffered in the interim. It is possible, though unlikely, that more Kentuckians might have joined Bragg's army, and/or that Bragg might have been able to force conscription on Kentuckians, thereby augmenting his army. While the Confederacy's long-term odds of success were not good, keeping Kentucky under Rebel control, even for a few months longer, would certainly have affected the outcome of the Civil War by delaying the capture of Chattanooga and the resulting Atlanta Campaign. Who knows?[32]

Buell Appoints "Maj. Gen." Charles Gilbert to Third Corps Command

Situation

As noted above, Maj. Gen. William Nelson was a very large, profane man with virtually no regard for the feelings of his subordinates. He had no patience for anything less than the immediate carrying out of his many orders, and he often cursed at those who failed in this task. As a result, he quickly

Brig. Gen. Jefferson C. Davis, USA. *The Photographic History of the Civil War, Vol. X.*

made enemies and discouraged friendships. Nelson blamed the Indiana soldiers for the debacle at Richmond, Kentucky, engendering their mutual disgust with him.[33]

One general Nelson quickly came to despise was Brig. Gen. Jefferson C. Davis of Indiana, whom he deemed a mere lackey of Maj. Gen. Horatio Wright, commanding at Cincinnati. On September 25, 1862, Nelson concluded that Davis had not worked hard enough to adequately prepare the defenses at Louisville. Nelson and Davis engaged in a shouting match, and in the aftermath, Nelson ordered Davis arrested and had him sent back to Indiana. Wright, not a fan of Nelson, ordered Davis to return to Kentucky but to avoid Nelson if at all possible.[34] Unfortunately, on the morning of September 29, Davis and several others saw Nelson in the lobby of the Galt House Hotel in Louisville. Davis started an argument with Nelson. Nelson ordered the "damned puppy" Davis to leave his sight. Davis then threw a hotel business card in Nelson's face, and Nelson slapped Davis in the face. Furious, Davis obtained a pistol, followed Nelson as he walked away, and fatally shot him in the chest.[35]

Maj. Gen. Don Carlos Buell had suddenly lost one of his proposed corps commanders. He needed to replace Nelson immediately, as he was already preparing to march on Bragg's army. Maj. Gen. George H. Thomas was to relieve Buell that same day, but Thomas refused the position.[36]

Options

Buell had two realistic options to replace Nelson as his proposed Third Corps commander: Brig. Gen. Albin F. Schoepf and "Maj. Gen." Charles Gilbert.[37]

Option 1

Schoepf gained experience as an officer in the Austrian army until he had defected to the Hungarian rebel forces during the revolutions of 1848. He had previously served as a corps commander, and he had fought at the Battles of Wildcat Mountain and Mill Springs. Thus Schoepf was the obvious choice based on experience. However, from Buell's perspective Schoepf was a strong supporter of Thomas and had come to despise Buell. Buell did not need another enemy in high command.[38]

Option 2

Buell's other choice was a most interesting character. West Point graduate Charles C. Gilbert had fought in the war with Mexico and gained additional experience through further assignments at West Point and in the Southwest. As a captain, he led a company of regular troops and had been wounded at the Battle of Wilson's Creek. In addition, Gilbert had served as inspector general

Acting Maj. Gen. Charles Gilbert, USA. *The Photographic History of the Civil War, Vol. X.*

of the Army of the Ohio at Shiloh and Corinth before accompanying Nelson to Kentucky. With Nelson wounded at the Battle of Richmond, Wright needed to replace him. When logical replacements Brig. Gens. Charles Cruft and James K. Jackson refused the assignment, Wright, on Cruft's and Jackson's suggestion, quickly recognized Gilbert's experience. Without any legal authority to do so, Wright promoted Gilbert to "acting major general" and placed him in command of Nelson's former troops. President Lincoln would ensure Gilbert was appointed to the rank of brigadier general. However, the Senate never confirmed his commission, so he was never a true major general. Holding (supposedly) enough rank, Gilbert was eligible for corps command.[39]

Decision

Buell appointed Gilbert to command the Third Corps.[40]

Results/Impact

Although a West Pointer and a seasoned soldier, Gilbert quickly proved to be a martinet whom his men despised. Further, he was grossly inexperienced for his new position, and he failed to display the necessary command ability. The end result of Nelson's death was that at the Battle of Perryville, Nelson was no longer in command of the Third Corps, that function having been assigned to Gilbert.[41]

During the Battle of Perryville, Gilbert remained passive as ordered (which will be discussed in relation to another critical decision). Even though he easily observed attacks against the First Corps on his immediate left, he sent that unit virtually no assistance. Gilbert's Corps left attacks on the First Corps by Cleburne, Anderson, and Powell almost completely unhindered. Brig. Gen. Philip Sheridan, beside himself with not being allowed to join the fray, took some action. As a result, the Battle of Perryville became a Confederate victory.[42]

Alternate Scenario

While many of Nelson's subordinates and soldiers might have hated him, his nature was such that he would have been highly unlikely to remain out of the Battle of Perryville. As soon as he either saw or was notified of the Confederate attacks moving across his front on the Springfield Road, he would have sent his men into action regardless of Buell's orders not to attack until the next day. This measure might well have prompted the Union Third Corps to attack and roll up what was present of Bragg's army's left flank, in particular Cleburne's, Anderson's, and Powell's attacking troops.[43]

Nelson's men might have defeated and even annihilated a good portion of Bragg's army, changing the rest of the Kentucky Campaign as we know it. Kirby Smith and what remained of Bragg's men would have had no choice but to retreat. Aggressively pursued by Nelson, both Bragg's and Kirby Smith's armies would have been forced into immediate retreat from Kentucky, probably suffering further losses, not to mention the loss of Kentucky even sooner than it occurred. Nelson's death had huge ramifications for the conduct and result of the Battle of Perryville.[44]

Bragg Unites with Kirby Smith and Assumes Command of Both Armies

Situation

Kirby Smith quickly broke the mutual agreement he and Bragg had accepted at Chattanooga on July 31. Determined to obtain glory, Kirby Smith quickly marched into Kentucky to throw off the burden of Union control on that state's supposed majority of Confederate citizens aching for freedom. He had somewhat irresponsibly insisted on leading his own campaign into Kentucky, and he made this decision based on optimistic reports from Col. John H. Morgan, his cavalry commander. Kirby Smith's success in winning the Battle of Richmond only confirmed that he was doing his part to liberate Kentucky from the Union.[45]

Arriving in Bardstown, Bragg received a letter from Kirby Smith effectively informing him that Kirby Smith's troops would be marching east to confront Union Brig. Gen. George W. Morgan's cavalry advancing north from Cumberland Gap, and with Brig. Gen. Humphrey Marshall's three thousand troops at Mount Sterling. Obviously, Kirby Smith had no interest in joining Bragg at this time and becoming his subordinate.[46] Bragg was already looking into the future of his campaign. The response of Kentucky men enlisting in his army had been mediocre at best: scarcely 1,500 had volunteered, and they were keen on joining the cavalry, not the infantry. As a result, the campaign seemingly was taking a different direction than planned.[47]

Options

At this point in time Bragg had three options: departing Bardstown with his army and attempting to flank Buell's force as it staggered toward Louisville, moving to Lexington and placing Kirby Smith firmly under his command, or establishing his army in a defensible position and awaiting a Union advance.[48]

Option 1

Having initially decided to move his troops to Bardstown, if Bragg acted quickly he might be able to interdict Buell's ragtag army as it advanced to Louisville. Bragg might still be able to harm the Federals and threaten Louisville itself. While Buell's army was not capable of organized resistance at this point, time was quickly running out for this to be a viable option.[49]

Option 2

Kirby Smith's refusal to join up with Bragg was no longer a good plan. Bragg could personally visit his junior officer and establish command over him and his small army. A unified force would be stronger and more likely to successfully confront an opposing Union army.[50]

Option 3

While Kirby Smith continued to avoid joining his army with Bragg's, Bragg could discover and position his army in a good, defensible location, accumulate supplies, and prepare to repel a Union effort to eject his army from Kentucky.[51]

Decision

Quickly realizing that it was too late to have much effect on Buell's straggling soldiers, on September 28 Bragg opted to meet Kirby Smith and establish command over him and his army. Bragg placed his own soldiers under the temporary command of Lieut. Gen. Leonidas Polk and rode to Lexington, arriving on October 1. While Kirby Smith was undoubtedly not pleased, consolidation of the two Rebel armies nonetheless became a reality.[52]

Results/Impact

With the addition of Brig. Gen. Carter Stevenson's division from Cumberland Gap to again augment Kirby Smith's small army, Bragg regained control of Cleburne's and Smith's Brigades. With a beefed-up command, Bragg prepared to deal with Buell or whatever Union forces that would move against him. Confident in his increased numbers, Bragg would soon open the Battle of Perryville, initially a Confederate victory. Yet before doing so, he had something else to accomplish.[53]

Alternate Scenario

Had Bragg decided not to force Kirby Smith and his army to fall under his command, he would have certainly become more leery of any Union troops sent to challenge his presence in Kentucky. However, Bragg felt no compunction about positioning his army at Perryville without Kirby Smith's assistance and fighting the Battle of Perryville. Although he won the battle, Bragg quickly realized he was outnumbered, then retreated. Somewhat ironically, the alternate scenario might well have had the same result as Bragg's critical decision.[54]

Buell Decides to Confront Bragg

Situation

Even as his ragtag soldiers trickled into Louisville, Buell knew that he needed to swiftly reconstitute his army before losing command of it. Yet he already had lost authority over his troops. Over a third of them immediately went AWOL (absent without leave), while many of those remaining in town defied regulations and proceeded to become drunk and disorderly. Only after several days did the army gradually settle down as it was resupplied and refitted. Joined by new recruits, Buell's men began to appear like an army once again. Buell knew that he must move aggressively againt the Rebel forces in Kentucky or lose his command.[55]

Long dissatisfied with Buell, the Lincoln administration took immediate action to relieve him as commander and replace him with a more competent and responsive officer. Therefore, on September 24 secret orders were forwarded to Louisville naming Maj. Gen. George H. Thomas as Buell's replacement. These orders were contingent upon Buell's continuing failure to conduct maneuvers against Bragg. Thomas was counseled to conduct "energetic operations," indicating the Lincoln administration's displeasure with its former commander.[56] As previously noted, Thomas declined the position, citing Buell's preparations to advance against Bragg. Buell had received a reprieve from an unlikely source; Thomas apparently had reasons of his own for not wanting this command.[57]

Options

Buell could follow one of two courses of action at this point. First, he could move against Bragg's combined armies in Kentucky. Or he could move against Bragg's combined armies while also sending a diversionary force to confuse Bragg.[58]

Option 1

Buell's first option, which the Lincoln administration strongly encouraged, was to quickly march to confront Bragg and his combined armies somewhere in Kentucky. This option demanded results—Buell knew he would chance losing his command if he didn't act. However, he might not consider his army ready to maneuver, due to new recruits, and that fact would have to be taken into consideration.[59]

Option 2

Buell's other option was to confuse Bragg as to his intentions. While maneuvering his army's three revamped corps to confront Bragg, Buell could order a diversionary force to mislead Bragg as to where his true advance would be located. Keeping Bragg guessing about his movements would allow Buell to maneuver to better advantage.[60]

Decision

Buell quickly made the critical decision to advance into Kentucky within the next few days and confront Bragg and his armies in battle, sending Brig. Gen. Joshua W.Sill's and Brig. Gen. Ebenezer Dumont's divisions toward Frankfort as a diversion. [61]

Results/Impact

Acting with undue haste, Buell quickly set to work organizing his army and ordering supplies ready to move with him as he took the field. Specifically, he arranged his army into three corps, splitting his now twenty-five brigades among them. Buell tried to ensure that each brigade consisted of three veteran regiments and one brand-new, untested regiment, believing that the new men would learn valuable lessons from the veterans. However, the experienced men often took advantage of the new recruits by telling tall tales and stealing their equipment.[62]

In designating his corps commanders, Buell made a poor decision resulting in failure at the Battle of Perryville. Gilbert's appointment to corps command and his resulting performance at the Battle of Perryville was previously discussed. Buell's plan to send Sill's and Dumont's divisions as a diversion for Bragg succeeded with Bragg eventually expecting to fight the battle for control of Kentucky near Frankfort as opposed to Perryville. This diversion fooled Bragg and resulted in the Battle of Perryville.[63]

Alternate Scenario

Had Thomas accepted command as was his due, chances are he would have delayed his advance against Bragg a few days. However, once Thomas decided it was time for battle (the Battle of Nashville), or was confronted with it (the Battle of Chickamauga), he proved to be an aggressive commander and a winner.[64]

Thomas would have been more likely to know of Bragg's location, and once confronted at what became the Battle of Perryville, he might well have moved to the front and directed the fighting himself. Though such assertions are speculative, Thomas could well have flanked Bragg's partial army at that battle as Brig. Gen. Philip H. Sheridan desired. He might also have turned the battle into a solid Union victory, quickly dashing Rebel hopes for further gains in Kentucky.[65]

Finally, following Lincoln's desire, Thomas might have been more effective at pursuing Bragg's and Kirby Smith's retreat through eastern Kentucky and even into East Tennessee. These actions would have continued to be detrimental to Rebel objectives.[66]

Bragg Installs a Confederate Governor at Frankfort

Situation

As noted above, Bragg had successfully reunited with Kirby Smith and now retained control of both invading armies. This larger command would increase the odds of success in future Rebel advances and maneuvering. However, Bragg had devised a new plan of attack without attacking.[67]

By this time in the campaign, Bragg had realized that male Kentuckians were not interested in rallying to the Rebel cause. If Confederate governance was established, the Confederacy could "legally" begin conscription efforts to enroll Kentucky men who had thus far been reluctant to enlist. While President Davis desired the formal "inauguration" of Richard Hawes, Kentucky's Confederate governor, Bragg saw an opportunity to quickly and "legally" augment his command by giving all Kentuckians the opportunity to join up.[68]

Options

Bragg faced with two options: he could take time to officially install Hawes as the Confederate governor of Kentucky, or he could bypass this installation and focus on a plan to defeat whatever Union forces were planning, or already moving, to confront his army.[69]

Option 1

Because of Kentuckians' poor response to the Confederate cause , Bragg had devised a plan to stimulate recruiting. He could install the provisional Confederate governor of Kentucky, Richard Hawes, in the capitol at Frankfort in an elaborate ceremony. Once Confederate rule was established, it would become lawful (from the Confederate viewpoint) to impose a draft on the state's men. Hopefully, this threatened draft would encourage volunteers to join Bragg's army. Perhaps this plan would also help solidify solidarity within the Confederate population? However, this scheme would leave Bragg less time to efficiently guide and concentrate his various divisions to address Union reaction to his invasion.[70]

Option 2

Bragg knew that the Lincoln administration would not tolerate a Rebel army marching at will throughout Kentucky without at least some kind of confrontation. Time, not an upscale formal installation of the governor, was of the essence in preparing for this encounter.[71]

Decision

Bragg installed Governor Hawes on October 4 at Frankfort, regardless of Union movements.[72]

Results/Impact

While still meeting with Kirby Smith on October 2, Bragg first learned that Brig. Gen. Joshua W. Sill's and Brig. Gen. Ebenezer Dumont's divisions were advancing toward the capitol at Frankfort. This knowledge should have quickly thwarted any plans for Hawes's formal inauguration. However, Bragg had made up his mind. Insisting the inauguration had to be held as scheduled, he rejected pleas to cancel the ceremony.[73]

Bragg arrived in Frankfort on October 3 and conducted the inauguration the next day as planned. Hawes took no oath as he had done several months earlier, but he delivered an address. As he finished speaking, artillery fire was heard in the distance. Only twelve miles away, Sill's and Dumont's divisions were quickly closing in on Frankfort, and that city had to be immediately abandoned. So much for the inauguration! Bragg's failure to install Hawes demonstrated to the Kentuckians that the Confederates were not in charge of the states political destiny. To focus on Hawes's installation, Bragg forewent planning an offense and gathering information on Buell's whereabouts. As a result of spending his time on the essentially wasted inauguration of Hawes, Bragg moved and attacked Buell at Perryville. The Confederate commander was unaware of the potentially dire situation looming there for some of his troops.[74]

Old Capitol Building, Frankfort, Kentucky. Photo by the author.

Alternate Scenario

Had Bragg decided to forego the inauguration of Governor Hawes, he would have been more prepared to deal with Sill's divisions as they advanced toward Frankfort. Further, Bragg might have been able to reassess other Union troop movements in hopes of determining who was marching where.[75] Additionally, he could have saved himself and the entire Confederacy an embarrassing incident. Bragg might have been able to prolong his stay in Kentucky, but not likely by more than a few days.[76]

CHAPTER 5

THE BATTLE OF PERRYVILLE, OCTOBER 8, 1862

The Battle of Perryville in and of itself certainly contained some critical decisions. However, viewing the battle from the perspective of the overall campaign, the result of the battle becomes our focus and not so much the actual fighting. In the future this series might well include a book on the critical decisions of the Battle of Perryville, examining it in more detail, as it certainly deserves. Here, we must focus on the battle within the context of the campaign, and, specifically, what effect it had on the final outcome. Likewise battles within other campaigns may well be examined.

The advance of both Maj. Gen. Edmund Kirby Smith's and Gen. Braxton Bragg's armies into Kentucky in the late summer of 1862 had forced the Union war effort to counter this so far successful campaign. After Buell's tattered army straggled into Louisville, he quickly ensured its rapid refitting and rebuilding. Knowing that his status as commander was in jeopardy, Buell wasted little time in advancing to confront Bragg's army. The result was the Battle of Perryville, sometimes labeled the "Gettysburg of the West" or the western Confederacy's "high water mark." While these epithets might be a bit of an overstatement, this battle nonetheless effectively ended Rebel hopes for Kentucky's becoming a true Confederate state. The Battle of Perryville perhaps represented the Confederacy's highest hopes for success in the Western theater. Four critical decisions affected the ensuing Battle of Perryville.

Bragg Orders Polk to Attack a Union Corps at Perryville

Situation

Maj. Gen. Don Carlos Buell, aware that the Lincoln administration was demanding quick and successful results, mobilized his Army of the Ohio as soon as he had seen to its refitting. Bragg was surprised to discover that by October 2, Buell's army was advancing toward Shelbyville. It was now Bragg's turn to respond.[1]

Buell was in fact advancing with his three corps, but not toward Shelbyville as Bragg's scouts had determined. Buell's First Corps, commanded by Maj. Gen. Alexander McDowell McCook, initially marched to Taylorsville, while Brig. Gen. (Acting Maj. Gen.) Charles C. Gilbert's Second Corps advanced directly toward Bardstown. Buell's Third Corps, commanded by Maj. Gen. Thomas L. Crittenden, also advanced toward Bardstown by way of Shepherdsville. Bragg was correct in believing that Buell's army was marching to Taylorsville. The Union commander had assigned a diversionary force consisting of two divisions of the First Corps led by Brig. Gen. Joshua W. Sill to march to the town and convince Bragg that it was the leading command of Buell's army.[2]

Bragg took the bait. Since Bragg was advancing to Frankfort, to conduct the inauguration, on October 2 he ordered Lieut. Gen. Leonidas Polk to advance from Bardstown and assault what he believed to be the main Union advance (Sill's command) on its right flank as it approached Frankfort. Whether the Federals' approach indicated merely reconnaissance or the advance of Buell's army, a successful assault could prove extremely beneficial for Bragg. However, Polk refused to obey this order and remained with his wing at Bardstown. Arriving in Frankfort on the evening of the third, Bragg received word from Polk of a possible Union concentration toward Bardstown. On October 4, Polk and the Army of the Mississippi took up the march, Hardee's wing toward Harrodsburg and Polk's wing toward Springfield and Danville. Polk notified Bragg that it was "inexpedient" to move on Sill. Bragg was still unaware of Buell's overall movements. As the Rebels marched east, they passed through the small town of Perryville.[3]

Hardee and his men stopped in Perryville to provide a barrier to Buell's advancing force and the supplies at Camp Dick Robinson. More importantly, due to the severe drought, water was extremely scarce, and one of the few sources was near Perryville within Doctor's Creek and the Chaplin River. Polk also sent his men back to Perryville to support Hardee. Polk erroneously stated to Bragg, "I cannot think it large," concerning the Union force near Perryville.[4]

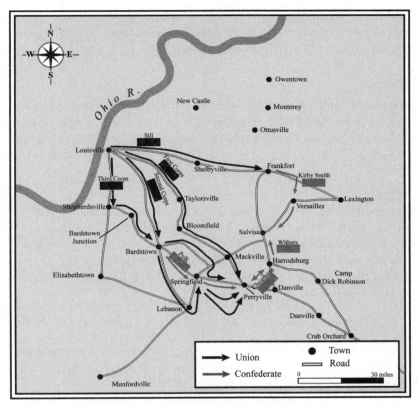

Union and Confederate Advance to Perryville, October 1–7, 1862

Options

Bragg had three options to choose from at this time. He could continue to have his army retreat until it joined physically with Kirby Smith's army. Then again, Bragg could turn and fight the advancing Union army, or he could disperse both Rebel armies until he was more informed of Yankee plans.[5]

Option 1

Although perhaps unaware of the Union Army of the Ohio's size, Bragg nonetheless realized that a significant force was marching in his direction, intent on forcing battle. Bragg determined that it might be best to combine the two Rebel armies in Kentucky to increase the odds of success against Buell's army. If separated, these two Confederate armies were more likely to be attacked one by one. However, Kirby Smith was extremely reluctant to give up his independent command and serve under Bragg.[6]

Option 2

Another option was for Bragg to utilize his army, under his direct command, to turn and engage Buell's men, hopefully on terrain benefiting the Rebels. This choice might well catch the Yankees off guard and give Bragg the benefit of surprise.[7]

Option 3

Bragg could also advance his two armies east until he could locate and prepare a strong defensive position of his choosing. Combined Rebel armies on the defense would potentially place Buell at a disadvantage, forcing him to assault a well-prepared and dug-in foe. The problem with this option might be that Buell could avoid battle and attempt to cut off Bragg's supplies as well as his line of retreat.[8]

Decision

Although Bragg was not present with Polk and Hardee, he made the critical decision to turn and give battle to the Union forces at Perryville. This led to the battle which occurred at Perryville.[9]

Results/Impact

The Battle of Perryville resulted from Bragg's critical decision. Fought on October 8, it ended in a tactical Confederate victory in the sense that the Yankees were forced back, and the Rebels held the field at the end of the day. However, as described below, the Confederates would quickly decide to retreat.[10]

Alternate Scenario

Had Bragg had better intelligence, he probably would not have ordered this attack against a much superior force consisting of three strong Federal corps. With this knowledge, Bragg would likely have continued to retreat until he could unite his forces and assume the defensive. Thus the Battle of Perryville would not have been fought. The confrontation would possibly have taken place farther east, casting another Kentucky town into the limelight.[11]

Buell Delays the Attack on the Confederates at Perryville until October 9

Situation

Buell's advance into Kentucky included four avenues of approach. He ordered Sill to march two divisions of the First Corps via Shelbyville directly toward the Kentucky capital at Frankfort to divert Bragg's attention. Meanwhile, Buell's three corps would march into Kentucky on different routes farther south. The First Corps, under the command of Maj. Gen. Alexander McD. McCook, would advance southeast via Taylorsville, Bloomfield, and Mackville, almost reaching Perryville. Taking a slightly more southern route, the Second Corps, under the command of Maj. Gen. Thomas L. Crittenden, would march through Mount Washington to Bardstown (where Bragg's army rested), Springfield, and then Lebanon and Perryville. Buell's Third Corps, commanded by Acting Maj. Gen. Charles C. Gilbert, would march south to Shepherdsville, then southeast to Bardstown, Springfield, and then toward Perryville. Maj. Gen. George Thomas was appointed second-in-command and accompanied the Second Corps.[12]

Kentucky was suffering from a prolonged drought at this time, and water proved very scarce for the Yankees as they advanced. The soldiers quickly wore themselves out searching for water sources from which they scrounged what they could.[13] McCook learned from Buell that Bragg had abandoned Bardstown and was apparently retreating toward Danville. Buell ordered McCook to march to Harrodsburg and join with Sill's two divisions. However, when he discovered that Sill was not yet at Frankfort, Buell changed McCook's orders. McCook was now to march via Mackville to Perryville, with Sill to follow and join him.[14]

Col. John H. Wharton's cavalry confronted Crittenden's Second Corps near Mount Washington. Pushing ahead, Crittenden's men marched through Bardstown and Springfield, constantly searching for any available water. They continued to advance toward Perryville via the Lebanon Pike. Gilbert's Third Corps also marched through Bardstown and Springfield, and then continued to Perryville.[15] Keeping ahead of Buell's three corps, Bragg's army retreated east, arriving at Perryville. Bragg decided early on October 7 to march his army north of the Kentucky River and unite with Kirby Smith's troops. Meanwhile, Hardee prepared to tangle with his pursuers, positioning his force facing west, just north of the town itself.[16]

Although Buell had ordered all three corps to advance on the morning of October 8, none of them were where he wanted them to be. Delay and procrastination had resulted in Buell's belief that it would take much of the day just to get his rear brigades into the Perryville area.[17]

Options

At this point, three options presented themselves to Buell: He could order an immediate attack on the Rebels at Perryville, or he could order an attack the next day, when all of his army was present. The third alternative was for Buell to order his corps to avoid battle and attempt to outflank Bragg.[18]

Option 1

Buell's combined corps significantly outnumbered Bragg's army, which still had not joined Kirby Smith's. Therefore, even without all his divisions present, Buell's forces nominally outnumbered Bragg's. The Union commander could continue to order those divisions into some semblance of a line of battle, and he could continue to advance on the brigades and divisions Bragg had confronting him.[19]

Option 2

Another option for Buell was simply to call off the proposed advance into battle until the next day. This choice would allow him to position most, if not all, of his divisions in a line of battle to confront Bragg's army. Of course, by giving himself an extra day, Buell assumed that Bragg would remain in place awaiting a Union advance.[20]

Option 3

Buell could collect his various scattered divisions and, rather than directly assaulting Bragg's force, attempt to outflank it. This option would cut off Bragg's supply line and connection with Kirby Smith's army, and it would ensure victory with potentially far fewer casualties for the Union army.[21]

Decision

Around 11:00 a.m., Buell chose to postpone his planned attack at Perryville until the next morning, when he would have most of his men in position for battle.[22]

Results/Impact

This critical decision had a most important impact on the resulting Battle of Perryville. Essentially, the fighting occurred between the force Bragg had in position at Perryville and the First Corps of Buell's army; the other two corps mostly sat out the battle under orders not to attack until the next morning. As a result, Bragg's smaller army actually defeated the First Corps and received credit for winning the Battle of Perryville. These Confederates were named the victors even though they had to almost immediately surrender the battlefield and withdraw when Bragg finally realized he was facing all three of Buell's corps, not just one.[23]

Alternate Scenario

Buell could have won the resulting battle had he continued his movements to confront Bragg's army on the eighth. Divisions such as Brig. Gen. Philip Sheridan's were well positioned to attack and roll up Bragg's left flank at maneuvered in battle, forcing him to retreat from the battlefield.[24]

Bragg Realigns His Divisions and Attacks

Situation

While Buell was preparing his various divisions and corps for a coordinated attack against Confederates at Perryville, Bragg faced a similar situation. Bragg was deceived into believing that most of Buell's army was advancing north of Perryville and threatening Kirby Smith's army around the small town of Salvisa. Thus Bragg ordered Polk, commanding at Perryville in his stead, to attack the presumedly small Union force discovered in the town early on October 8. Remember that these Federals sought water, found in some abundance in nearby Doctor's Creek and Chaplin River.[25]

Bragg vacillated and then decided that, while a significant Union presence had already been revealed at Perryville, enemy troops were not present at or near Salvisa. Therefore, he ordered Polk to attack the Union force at Perryville early on the eighth. Meanwhile, on the evening of October 7, Hardee wrote a dispatch to Bragg explaining in pedantic detail that he should not divide his army in the face of battle. Polk also sent a dispatch to Bragg, who received it en route to Perryville around 7:00 a.m. on the eighth, declaring that he would attack "vigorously" that morning. However, Bragg and his staff heard no loud sounds of battle as they made their way toward Perryville.[26]

Bragg arrived as fighting at Peter's Hill faded. Sheridan tried to get water for his men, but Gilbert (not a fighting commander like Nelson) recalled him for advancing too early. Bragg quickly realized that Polk's command was ill positioned for combat. Polk had held a conference with his senior commanders,

Maj. Gen. Leonidas Polk, CSA. *The Photo-graphic History of the Civil War, Vol. X.*

and "they" had decided to "adopt the defensive-offensive" instead of attacking as Bragg had ordered.[27]

Options

As Bragg resumed command, he was faced with three options: ordering an assault with the various brigades positioned as they were, realigning his divisions and brigades into a more suitable configuration, or ordering a retreat to a more defensible location, possibly combining his army with Kirby Smith's.[28]

Option 1

Bragg could order the brigades to attack from their positions north of Perryville. However, he observed that his right flank was vulnerable, and he knew he would have to maintain due vigilance concerning this potential problem.[29]

Option 2

Observing his right flank's susceptibility to assault, Bragg could realign his command in order to protect it. However, this process would take several hours to complete, and he was unsure just what maneuvering the opposing Union force might conduct in the meantime.[30]

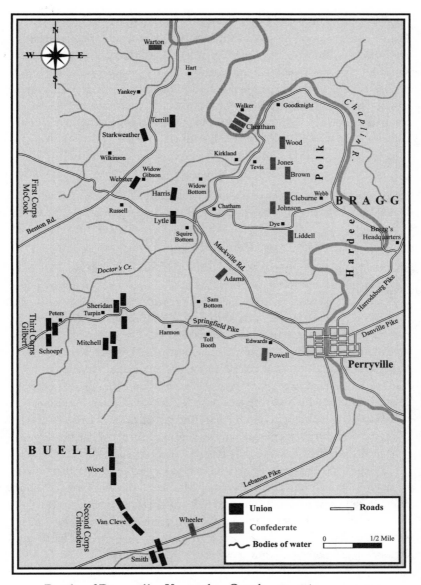

Battle of Perryville, Kentucky, October 8, 1862, 2:00 P.M.

Option 3

Rather than exposing his command to Yankee assault(s) during the realignment process, Bragg could order an orderly withdrawal or retreat. Doing so would cost him potentially no casualties, and it would also allow him to choose a more defensible nearby location to resist an onslaught. This option would assume that the Federal command would cooperate and not hinder the withdrawal. In addition, it would likely only postpone Bragg's eventual confrontation with all or part of Buell's army.[31]

Decision

Bragg quickly chose to realign his command before ordering an assault on the Union force in place, all while protecting his right flank.[32]

Results/Impact

The results of this critical decision were the Rebel assault on McCook's First Corps and the Battle of Perryville as we know it today. Bragg pulled Maj. Gen. Benjamin F. Cheatham's division out of its present position and marched it north to Walker's Bend in the Chaplin River. Wharton's cavalry maintained vigilance on this flank, observing more Union troops moving east but not outflanking Bragg's army. Once Cheatham's Division was in position, Bragg ordered the advance. Cheatham's Division quickly came under heavy fire, but it managed to conduct successful assaults on McCook's left, capture Lieut. Charles Parson's battery, and push McCook's brigades back some distance as they were brought into the fray. The rest of Bragg's divisions assisted in this effort with further assaults. The failure of Buell's other two corps to engage in the fighting allowed the Rebels temporary success.[33]

A large contribution to Bragg's success was a phenomenon called "acoustic shadow," which was a trick played by Mother Nature whereby the sounds of battle somehow were not conveyed to Buell's headquarters. Thus Buell did not learn until much later in the day that a battle was even being fought! The acoustic shadow, along with his orders to postpone the proposed battle until October 9, gave Bragg unknown assistance in his victory.[34]

Alternate Scenario

Had Bragg assaulted the Union divisions present without realigning Cheatham's Division, the elements of McCook's Corps might have outflanked Bragg's right while forcing parts of the Third Corps into the battle. These actions could have resulted in a Federal victory and forced Bragg to initiate a retreat from Kentucky even sooner than the actual one. A Union victory here would certainly have ended all concerns over Confederate retention of Kentucky.[35]

Bragg Retreats from Perryville

Situation

As night settled over the Perryville Battlefield, the fighting finally halted. Bragg's troops had fought well. His relatively small command had forced McCook's Corps back almost a mile, but it had managed to regroup and form a line of defense. Bragg had won the day but at significant cost. Per his initial estimate, he had lost 30 percent of his men on the battlefield.[36]

At his headquarters in the Crawford house, Bragg learned from Wheeler, who had bravely held off Crittenden's Second Corps all afternoon on the Lebanon Pike, southwest of Perryville, that that corps was indeed present. Other information indicated that many more Federal units were either on the battlefield or close by. Bragg worried that in spite of his victory, his army might be susceptible to an assault on the morrow.[37]

Options

At this time Bragg could choose from three options. He could remain on the battlefield and continue to do battle with the Union force, such as it was, the next day. A second course of action involved withdrawing his force and arranging a rendezvous with Kirby Smith's army. Lastly, Bragg could retreat to a more defensible position to confront Buell's united army.[38]

Option 1

Bragg was supposedly in a position to renew the fighting the next morning. His commanders and men were flush with a hard-earned victory. However, Bragg was beginning to realize that he would likely confront most, if not all, of Buell's army. A force of this size would significantly reduce the odds of further victory.[39]

Option 2

Perhaps a much safer course of action would be for Bragg to withdraw while he could and unite with Kirby Smith's army. This choice would increase his total manpower and allow for better odds in another confrontation with Buell's troops.[40]

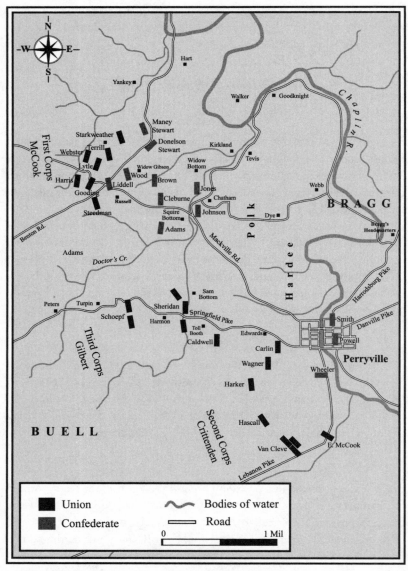

Battle of Perryville, Kentucky, October 8, 1862, 8:00 P.M.

Option 3

Bragg's other consideration was that if Buell had most or all of his army present, he could take the initiative and attempt to outflank Bragg, cutting him off from his supply depots farther east at Camp Dick Robinson near Bryantsville. This action would place Bragg in dire straits. He knew that the loss of his army would be unacceptable to the Rebel high command.[41]

Decision

Quickly making up his mind, Bragg withdrew his army to Harrodsburg, where it would unite with Kirby Smith's army, forming a larger combat power.[42]

Results/Impact

The withdrawal began shortly after midnight. By early morning, Bragg's entire force was marching toward Harrodsburg. Bragg was deeply concerned that Buell would quickly pursue, but that did not occur. The acoustic shadow and continuing problems with Buell's command combined to prevent his active pursuit. Quite the opposite, Buell's men expected to endure another day of hard fighting: all were surprised to learn of Bragg's leaving the battlefield.[43]

Alternate Scenario

Had Bragg remained to fight a second day, he could well have suffered a serious defeat, even with the reinforcement of Kirby Smith's army. A rout of the Rebels would have ended the Confederacy's hopes of retaining Kentucky.[44]

CHAPTER 6

RETREAT OUT OF KENTUCKY, OCTOBER 9–24, 1862

The Battle of Perryville became the defining battle of the Kentucky Campaign of 1862. Although he and his troops were technically the victors, Bragg wisely retreated before confronting Buell's additional two corps. By this point, Bragg had concluded that Kentuckians were not flocking to the Rebel cause and were unlikely to ever do so. They seemed to be more interested in preserving their livelihoods than in joining his army. A final critical decision by Bragg, followed by another one by Buell, ended the Kentucky Campaign of 1862.

Bragg Decides to Abandon Kentucky

Situation

After Gen. Braxton Bragg had marched his army to Harrodsburg, he decided to continue his withdrawal and retreat to safety farther east. As a result, when Maj. Gen. Edmund Kirby Smith arrived at Harrodsburg with his troops, he discovered that most of Bragg's army had already marched away! Bragg's men, followed by Kirby Smith's, retreated east to Camp Dick Robinson, where supplies awaited them.[1]

Bragg had developed a serious aversion to Kentucky, and especially to its male citizens by the time of the Battle of Perryville. Answering the siren call of Kentucky's Confederate-leaning citizens, he and Kirby Smith entered that state expecting to recruit thousands of individuals yearning to support their cause. Indeed, Bragg mentioned that he had transported some fifteen thousand rifle muskets to distribute to these new enlistees. Yet only a few thousand at the most actually volunteered, and most of these desired service in the cavalry, not in the infantry that needed them. Thus, few enlistments resulted.[2]

Bragg had several additional facts to consider before deciding what to do next. One concern was that his position at Camp Dick Robinson was predicated in part on its large accumulation of supplies. However, Bragg discovered less than a week's worth of provisions. The drought made foraging for additional food unlikely, and it also limited his sources of available water. Moreover, he seemed unlikely to receive additional reinforcements. In a battle for possession of Corinth, Maj. Gen. William S. Rosecrans had just defeated the combined armies of Maj. Gen. Earl Van Dorn and Maj. Gen. Sterling Price. After this loss, these troops would be unable to advance into Kentucky in support of Bragg. Another possible force in Tennessee under the command of Maj. Gen. John C. Breckinridge also failed to come to Bragg's assistance. As usual, rumors persisted of further Union reinforcements, led by Brig. Gen. Gordon Granger, headed in Bragg's direction. These reports turned out to be correct.[3]

Options

Bragg was now faced with two options: he could make a stand in or around Camp Dick Robinson, or he could retreat out of Kentucky.[4]

Option 1

Bragg could remain in Kentucky and attempt to hold on to the state for the Confederacy. He might be able to conscript some local men, but that was a tenuous possibility. Maintaining adequate supplies and ammunition for his combined army also appeared dubious. Additional Rebel reinforcements did not appear to be available.[5]

Option 2

Bragg's other option was to give up on holding the state and withdraw into Tennessee. Logistically he did not have much choice, but he knew that to retreat after a successful beginning to this campaign would cause outrage and disbelief within the Rebel high command, his own army, Kirby Smith's army, and the Confederacy in general.[6]

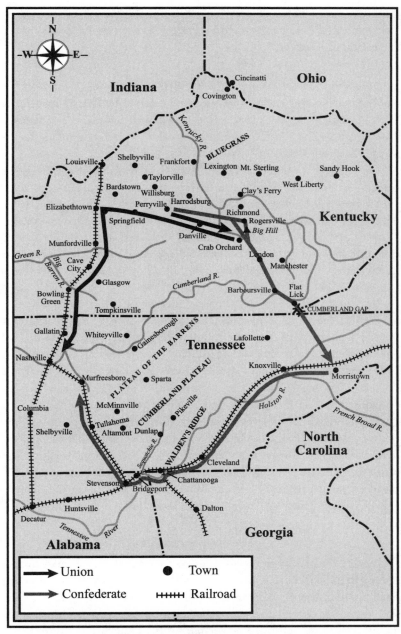

Bragg and Kirby Smith's Retreat out of Kentucky,
October 9–24, 1862

Decision

On October 12, Bragg announced his critical decision to abandon Kentucky and retreat to Knoxville.[7]

Results/Impact

Understandably, this decision was not well received by Bragg's officers and men. Dissension began to fester, especially among his senior commanders. However, Bragg had been backed into a situation whereby he did not see any way to remain in Kentucky.[8]

On October 13 the retreat began. For lack of available forage, Bragg decided to split the armies' routes: after reaching Lancaster, his troops would march via Crab Orchard and Mount Vernon, while Kirby Smith's would march via Paint Lick and London. The journey was a miserable one. Pvt. Sam Watkins of the First Tennessee famously described it as follows: "Tramp, tramp, tramp, and no sound or noise but the same inevitable, monotonous tramp, tramp, tramp, up hill and down hill, through long and dusty lanes, weary, worn-out and hungry."[9]

Watkins's description of the retreat was typical. It was a terrible time for both of the Rebel armies involved: foraging proved largely unsuccessful, the men suffered from hunger, and moving the wagon train up Big Hill proved trying. On October 20, the lead units began arriving at Morristown, Tennessee, where they boarded railroad cars that took them to Knoxville. At Knoxville, Bragg's troops were refitted with uniforms, and ample rations were distributed for the first time in weeks.[10]

Positioned south of Nashville around Murfreesboro and points east and west of that town, Bragg awaited a Federal advance in the following spring, once the roads became favorable for travel. He was therefore caught by surprise when Rosecrans, newly appointed commander of the Army of the Ohio, advanced the day after Christmas. This approach brought on the Battle of Stones River or Murfreesboro, and Confederate defeat.[11]

Alternate Scenarios

Had Bragg and Kirby Smith united and cooperated earlier, maneuvering against Buell as one army, Buell might well have suffered defeat. However, Buell had significantly more men, and he likely would have prevailed, possibly rendering Bragg's army incapable of further fighting, perhaps capturing most of those not killed or wounded. This result would not only save Kentucky for the Union, but also reduce or eliminate a major Confederate army.[12]

Had Buell's men aggressively conducted a turning maneuver and cut Bragg off from his line of retreat in inhospitable territory, Bragg might have been forced to surrender. His army would then have been eliminated as a factor for further combat—exactly what Jefferson Davis had advised him not to let happen. Of course, Bragg would have worked diligently not to become entrapped, and the inhospitable territory would have been equally problematic for Buell.[13]

Buell Marches to Nashville, Allowing Bragg and Kirby Smith to Escape

Situation

Once Buell ascertained that Bragg was retreating from Camp Dick Robinson, Bragg and Kirby Smith had somewhat of a head start. While he did round up some of Bragg's men, content to give up fighting, Buell was already significantly behind Bragg. The splitting of Bragg's and Kirby Smith's commands further complicated Buell's ability to pursue. Due to the drought, he was quite aware that he would have to provide his own food and forage, as little would be available in that region. In addition, Buell was conscious of the Lincoln administration's desire to capture eastern Tennessee.[14]

Options

Buell now had two options available to him. He could continue to pursue both Bragg's and Kirby Smith's armies, or he could maneuver elsewhere to re-engage Bragg's or some other Rebel army.[15]

Option 1

Under great pressure to somehow confront these two Rebel armies before they escaped Kentucky, as well as to advance into and protect eastern Tennessee, Buell knew what was expected of him. However, he was concerned about the lack of available supplies for his large army. He believed that it was impossible to keep his army fed (just as Bragg was discovering). Plus, Buell had no desire to wander about that comparatively desolate area in pursuit of the Rebel armies.[16]

Option 2

Buell's other option was to ignore the administration's demands and maneuver through much more favorable terrain to a new location—probably in or near Nashville—where he could confront Bragg. Rather than risk losing men in a futile pursuit, Buell could reposition his army where it could do the most good. Nashville seemed the most likely destination for Bragg's army; he could arrive ahead of his troops and protect the city.[17]

Decision

Ignoring the administration's wishes, Buell made the final critical decision of the Kentucky Campaign of 1862 by ordering his army to change course and advance on Nashville.[18]

Results/Impact

The results of this decision were not long in arriving. Bragg and Kirby Smith both escaped to fight another day. More importantly for Buell, he was quickly relieved of command on October 24 and replaced by Maj. Gen. William S. Rosecrans.[19] Washington would quickly hound Rosecrans to advance south of his Nashville camps and attack Bragg's army, which was dispersed around Murfreesboro. After heavy refitting of his army, Rosecrans finally did advance as requested. The Battle of Stones River or Murfreesboro, an eventual Union victory President Lincoln desperately needed, occurred as the result.[20]

Alternate Scenario

In light of what quickly resulted from refusing to travel farther east, Buell would probably have kept his command had he made some effort to pursue Bragg through eastern Kentucky and perhaps eastern Tennessee. In fact, Buell could well have retained his position regardless of that pursuit's success or failure. Both Lincoln and Halleck cautioned Buell that if Bragg could live off the land, so could he. By ignoring this advice, Buell lost his command.[21]

CHAPTER 7

AFTERMATH AND CONCLUSIONS

Many ramifications resulted from the successful retreat of the two Rebel armies. Looking at the big picture from Gen. Braxton Bragg's viewpoint, he was subsequently able to convince Confederate president Jefferson Davis that while he had done the best he could, the citizens of Kentucky would not effectively support him or his army. Davis accepted Bragg's story and kept him in command of the newly designated Army of Tennessee (the unit would be known by this name for the rest of the war). Bragg ordered these troops to advance to just south of Nashville, where they would spend the winter.[1]

However, few others visualized the campaign as anything other than a failure. Maj. Gen. Edmund Kirby Smith was vociferous in his criticism of Bragg, yet Bragg remained in command. In fact, Kirby Smith's small army was placed under his authority as a third corps. Despite his objections to President Davis, Bragg was forced to order one large division (Maj. Gen. Carter Stevenson's) to Vicksburg in December, and the remaining divisions were broken up and reassigned within Bragg's army. Kirby Smith was reassigned farther west.[2]

Bragg's commanders, as well as his men, generally criticized the results of the campaign. His senior commanders' displeasure would eliminate his ability to effectively utilize the Army of Tennessee as a fighting force. Bragg's handling of the Battle of Stones River or Murfreesboro only accelerated this trend.[3]

Maj. Gen. Don Carlos Buell fared worse. As he disregarded President Abraham Lincoln's specific desires to catch Bragg's army and move in and protect eastern Tennessee, Lincoln and Secretary of War Edwin Stanton quickly relieved him of command. Buell's replacement was Maj. Gen. William S. Rosecrans. After much waiting for the buildup of supplies, Rosecrans led the advance against Bragg at Stones River and successfully fought off Bragg's early morning assault.[4]

The Union's critical decisions may be summarized as follows: Halleck, an army and department commander, made one; Buell, an army commander, made six; Nelson, an army commander, made one; and Manson, a brigade commander, made one. The Rebels' critical decisions may be enumerated thusly: Davis, the Confederate president, made two; Bragg, an army and department commander, made ten and shared an eleventh with Kirby Smith; and Kirby Smith, an army and department commander, made five and shared a sixth with Bragg. (This is the first time I have encountered a shared critical decision.) Of the six categories of critical decisions, thirteen were strategic, seven were tactical, two were organizational, two were operational, one was logistical, and three were personnel related. At least one critical decision was made in each category. In this campaign, most such decisions were reached in the field, and few were made prior to the fighting.

What happened to Bragg and the Confederacy because of the Kentucky Campaign of 1862? Why was it unsuccessful? While the Kentucky Campaign was one of the lesser-known major campaigns of the Civil War, why aren't more Civil War buffs aware of it? Perhaps the Rebels' failure to gain and maintain any kind of grip on Kentucky and the resultant retreat of Bragg's combined armies to Tennessee presents the "nothing really changed" mentality?

The crux of the Rebel failure in this campaign was Davis's decision to keep Kirby Smith's Department of East Tennessee separate from Bragg's Department and Army of the Mississippi (what would eventually be named the Army of Tennessee). Had Bragg been afforded overall command from the beginning of the "arrangement" with Kirby Smith, would his combined force have been powerful enough to do battle with Buell's army and perhaps make a stronger statement of Confederate control of Kentucky? Either Davis or Bragg might have quickly clarified whether Kirby Smith would immediately fall under Bragg's command. Bragg might then have had the ability to confront Buell's army in Tennessee and render it ineffective before it escaped to Louisville. From then on, who knows how the campaign might have ended?

Kirby Smith's independent decision to march into Kentucky on his own, avoiding Cumberland Gap, altered Bragg's options as he launched his own campaign. Kirby Smith had no right to violate the agreement made with Bragg. Certainly Davis's critical decision to maintain two separate departments within Tennessee contributed to the problem. Unfortunately for the

Confederacy, Davis's penchant to continue the system of small departments scattered over the Confederacy ultimately contributed to the eventual failure of the Confederacy.

Gen. Braxton Bragg had to accept some of the responsibility for the campaign's failure. He initially failed to clarify with Davis whether or not he could command Kirby Smith in the field. In fact, Bragg should have demanded that responsibility when he became aware of Kirby Smith's apparent disregard for their agreement to cooperate.

Over time, Bragg became known as an extremely competent organizer of commands and armies. His logistical skills also drew praise. Yet once he began maneuvering in campaigns and battles, he seemed unable to react to his enemy's movements, especially if they were uexpected. Often his plan would fail to materialize, resulting in an eventual lack of success or victory. This fact became obvious to at least some of his subordinates, and they lost confidence in their commander, never a good thing for an army.

Once Kirby Smith decided to invade Kentucky on his own—not a helpful action for the future campaign—he did make several critical decisions with positive results. Bypassing Cumberland Gap saved him much time and many casualties. During his advance and fighting at Richmond, Kirby Smith made several beneficial critical decisions. One choice was brilliant: positioning Scott's cavalry north of Richmond, even as the battle was being fought, in order to capture Yankees fleeing from the battle he had not yet won. This action resulted in the capture of thousands of Union soldiers. However, while understandable, Kirby Smith's strong desire to remain in independent command as long as possible did place a significantly greater burden on Bragg, forcing him to continue to operate without Kirby Smith's additional troops. Had Kirby Smith cooperated with Bragg better and sooner, the campaign might have been marginally more successful.

Bragg conducted a very successful movement to transfer his army to Chattanooga. His initial audacious invasion of Kentucky provided a serious setback for the Union high command, causing major scrambling for soldiers and other resources to combat his troops. Then Bragg vacillated in making critical decisions about his army's next move. His soldiers' encirclement of Munfordville wasted time and distracted him from what he should have done, which was to confront Buell's army and defeat it. Had Kirby Smith accompanied Bragg, they might well have accomplished this feat.

Bragg made what many historians consider an unwise critical decision to install Richard Hawes as the Confederate governor of Kentucky. What Bragg should have been doing instead was monitoring Buell's location and attempting to divine his and his men's intentions. Hindsight wasn't required to reach this conclusion, as the sound of Union cannon fire interrupted the inauguration. This wasted time indicates Bragg's failure to understand Buell's strategy of advancing and engaging the Confederates in battle.

The saying "I'd rather be lucky than good" certainly applied to Bragg and his handling of the Battle of Perryville. After Polk decided not to attack immediately as ordered, Bragg arrived, repositioned his men, conducted a smart offense, and obtained a solid victory. Yet had Buell ordered his other two corps into battle that day instead of postponing their advance, Bragg likely would have suffered a severe defeat.

Bragg is usually faulted for giving up and leaving Kentucky. But did he really have a choice? He had access to less than a week's worth of supplies. His recruiting efforts had been mostly ineffective due to Kentucky men's reluctance to fight; the majority of eligible Kentuckians did not volunteer for military service. Moreover, Bragg's proposal to implement a Rebel draft was never fulfilled, as Governor Hawes was not allowed to remain in office after his inauguration. The draft's questionable enforceability only added to the difficulties. Also, Jefferson Davis had ordered Bragg not to lose his army in Kentucky, as it was too valuable a resource. Since Maj. Gens. Earl Van Dorn's and Sterling Price's combined armies had just lost to Rosecrans at Corinth, they were now unavailable to join Bragg's men in Kentucky. Similarly, Maj. Gen. John C. Breckinridge's division had been ordered to Holly Springs and could not join Bragg. Finally, Bragg had learned that Yankee reinforcements under Brig. Gen. Gordon Granger were en route to augment Buell, worsening the Confederates' odds of success in another battle.[5]

Several of Buell's critical decisions hurt his performance and caused his eventual removal. His failure to pursue and attack Bragg early in the campaign resulted in Buell's flight to Louisville. Buell then made the critical decision to advance against Bragg. However, two critical decisions cost Buell the Battle of Perryville. First, he appointed Acting Maj. Gen. Charles Gilbert to command his Third Corps, and Gilbert essentially sat out the battle. In contrast, Maj. Gen. William Nelson, the commander Gilbert replaced, would likely have joined the fighting had he not been murdered. Gilbert sat out the battle because Buell had made the critical decision to postpone the battle until the next day, October 9. Buell's final critical decision not to pursue Bragg during his retreat from Kentucky, and his disobedience of the Lincoln administration's orders to advance into eastern Tennessee and regain it for the Union cause, quickly caused his removal from command.

In summary, the Kentucky Campaign of 1862 initially put the Union on the defense in the Western Theater. Kirby Smith, taking advantage of additional troops loaned to him, immediately voided the new agreement with

Bragg and marched into Kentucky to liberate it. Nonetheless, he was initially successful, routing the Federal force at Richmond. Bragg quickly forced Buell to take the defense and react to the Rebels. Though Bragg's masterful movement of troops to Chattanooga clearly outmaneuvered Buell, the Rebels soon gave up the initiative, allowing Buell to escape back to Louisville. After regrouping and refitting there, the Union commander would return to confront Bragg. Bragg's critical decision to waste time ensuring the capture of Munfordville might be considered a turning point in the campaign.

Eligible Kentucky men's failure to join the Rebel ranks severely diminished the Confederacy's ability to hold the state. However, this lack of commitment was unanticipated, and it was not Bragg's fault. His wavering, his failure to order Kirby Smith's army to join his as originally agreed, and his lack of information on Buell's corps led to the only major battle in Kentucky. While the Battle of Perryville was technically a Confederate victory, the Rebels were lucky that more Union corps were not involved, indicating a significant error on Buell's part.

Although Kirby Smith blamed Bragg, Kirby Smith's initial failure to cooperate forced Bragg out on his own. Jefferson Davis added to the Confederates' difficulties by establishing two departments where one would have been more logical. Buell's initial failure to confront Bragg, coupled with his later failure to pursue Bragg, resulted in his removal.

Buell's march to Nashville, where Maj. Gen. William Rosecrans replaced him, set up the Battle of Stones River / Murfreesboro, which became a Union victory and gave President Lincoln the opportunity to activate his Emancipation Proclamation. While Bragg established a line south of Murfreesboro, Rosecrans refitted and also built up his cavalry. His ten-day Tullahoma Campaign in late June and early July quickly forced Bragg back to Chattanooga. At the end of the Chickamauga Campaign, Bragg defeated Rosecrans at the Battle of Chickamauga with the assistance of troops from Lee's army. However, Bragg failed to adequately pursue the Yankees back into Chattanooga. With Maj. Gen. Ulysses Grant now in command as Rosecrans's replacement, the tide quickly turned in the ensuing Battle of Chattanooga. The stage was then set for Maj. Gen. William T. Sherman's Atlanta Campaign, a Union advance that was a major turning point in the war. Sherman's March to the Sea drove a stake through the heart of the Confederacy, contributing significantly to its ultimate defeat.

The lesser-known Kentucky Campaign of 1862 initially provided the Confederacy potential for great success when it was highly desirable and needed. One can only wonder how different the campaign's outcome might have been had some of the critical decisions been made differently.

APPENDIX I

DRIVING TOUR OF THE CRITICAL DECISIONS OF THE 1862 KENTUCKY CAMPAIGN

In order to better understand where and why the critical decisions of the Kentucky Campaign of 1862 were made, the following driving tour is provided. There is no better way to grasp the enormity of a critical decision than to stand in the same location where it was made. However, it is not always worthwhile to reach every one of these sites. For instance, President Davis appointed Bragg to command of the Army of Tennessee while he was in Richmond, Virginia, a considerable distance from where the other critical decisions were made. Also, please realize that these stops are *not* part of a battle or campaign tour. Tours of battlefields can be found elsewhere.

Due to the extreme distances the Kentucky Campaign covered, mileages between stops are approximate. The total mileage, leaving and returning to Chattanooga, is about 773 miles. For comparison, Bragg's movement of his army from Tupelo to Chattanooga totaled 776 miles. Therefore, this journey will require some planning ahead. At each stop it will largely be up to you, the reader, to find appropriate specific tour guidance. Tours are readily available at some of these destinations. All of the standard safety rules apply, such as being careful while exiting your vehicle, crossing roads, etc.

The tour begins and ends in downtown Chattanooga. After leaving Chattanooga, you will travel through Knoxville and roughly follow Maj. Gen.

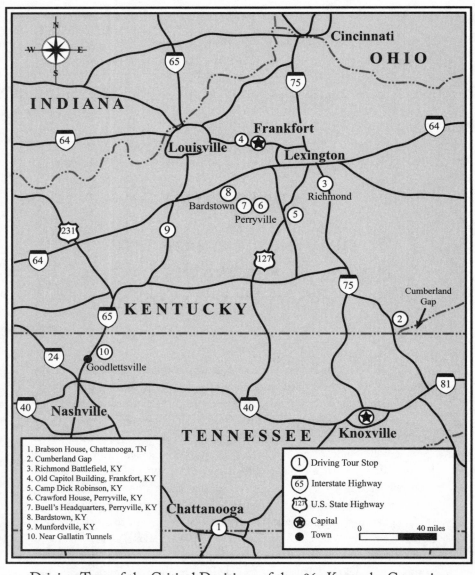

Driving Tour of the Critical Decisions of the 1862 Kentucky Campaign

Edmund Kirby Smith's advance to Cumberland Gap and then to Richmond, Kentucky. After several stops near Perryville, the tour maximizes mileage efficiency by generally tracing Bragg's advance into Kentucky in reverse. You may modify entries and exits and take in other sites if desired.

Please remember that, while some of these tour locations include parts of battlefields, this is a tour of the sites of critical decisions. You are welcome to combine locations for battlefields and critical decisions at your discretion.

Begin the tour by driving to 405 East Fifth Street in downtown Chattanooga. Park, and note the historical tablet marking the site of the Brabson House / Bragg's headquarters.

Stop 1—Bragg's Headquarters, Brabson House, Chattanooga

Critical Decisions: (1) Halleck Splits Up His Force at Corinth, (2) Davis Removes Beauregard and Places Bragg in Command, (3) Davis Places Chattanooga Within Kirby Smith's Department, (4) Kirby Smith Decides to Liberate Kentucky, (5) Bragg Decides to Beat Buell to Chattanooga, (6) Bragg and Kirby Smith Agree to Conduct a Joint Campaign, (11) Bragg Invades Kentucky, Bypassing Nashville, (15) Buell Decides to Retreat to Nashville

We will briefly discuss eight critical decisions, a few reached near here, and others made beyond the scope of the driving tour.

After Maj. Gen. Henry W. Halleck captured Corinth, he largely give up the important gains he had made. While in Corinth he decided to break up his command.

Narrative of Kenneth Noe,
Perryville: This Grand Havoc of Battle

Accordingly, Halleck made the worst decision of his career. Instead of continuing forward to Tupelo or Vicksburg, he divided his force and ceased advancing south at all. One division went to Arkansas to bolster Maj. Gen. Samuel Curtis's Federal forces in that state. Grant's Shiloh army—now under George Thomas's command—and most of Pope's army as well, dispersed in garrisons behind the lines, across healthier areas of the region. There, they would cover rail routes in the rear that were increasingly vital now that the Tennessee River finally was dropping. Inertia and debilitating illness followed in northern Mississippi and western Tennessee.[1]

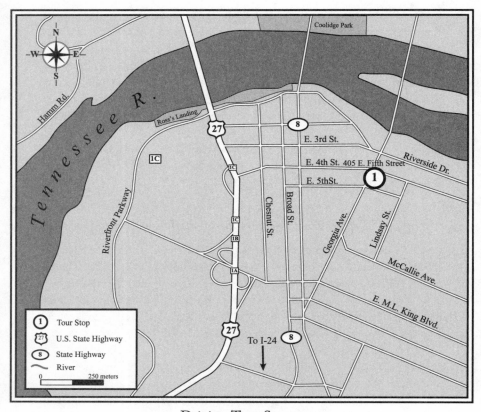

Driving Tour Stop 1,
Site of Brabson House, Chattanooga, TN

President Jefferson Davis did not like Gen. P. G. T. Beauregard. When the general left Tupelo for a few days to regain his deteriorating health, Davis replaced him with Gen. Braxton Bragg. Bragg would ultimately command the Kentucky Campaign of 1862.

Message from President Davis to Gen. Braxton Bragg

RICHMOND, VIRGINIA, June 20, 1862.
General BRAXTON BRAGG, Tupelo, Miss.:

Your dispatch informing me that General Beauregard had turned over the command to you and left for Mobile on surgeons certificate was duly received. You are assigned permanently to the command of the department, as will be more formally notified to you by the Secretary of War. You will correspond directly and receive orders and instructions from the Government in relation to your future operations.

JEFFERSON DAVIS[2]

Bragg believed that he was in command of Chattanooga, and he was therefore surprised to discover that he was a guest in Kirby Smith's Department of East Tennessee.

Message from Gen. Braxton Bragg to Maj. Gen. Edmund Kirby Smith

HEADQUARTERS DEPARTMENT No. 2,
Chattanooga, Tenn., August 8, 1862.
General E. KIRBY SMITH,
Comdg. Department of East Tennessee, Knoxville, Tenn.:
GENERAL:
By General Orders, No. 50, War Department, July 18, I find myself within the limits of your department. Without an explanation this might seem an unjustifiable intrusion but for your letter of the 24th ultimo, received by me in Montgomery, inviting me to make the move I was, then executing. The general order in question, which was duly received on the 6th~ instant, defines the eastern boundary of my department very differently from my previous instructions, copies of which are herewith. Under these I acted, and should feel much embarrassed in my present position but for the cordial manner in which you have offered cooperation, and indeed placed your command at my disposition. Neither of us have any other object than the success of our cause. I am satisfied no misunderstanding can occur from necessary union of our forces.

Respectfully and truly, general, your obedient servant,

BRAXTON BRAGG[3]

Upon receiving the message and follow-up below, Kirby Smith became extremely enthused about the probability of successfully invading Kentucky.

Message from Col. John H. Morgan
to Maj. Gen. Edmond Kirby Smith

GEORGETOWN, Ky., July 16, 1862.

General SMITH:

I am here with a force sufficient to hold all the country out-side of Lexington and Frankfort. These places are garrisoned chiefly with Home Guards. The bridges between Cincinnati and Lexing-ton have been destroyed. The whole country can be secured, and 25,000 or 30,000 men will join you at once. I have taken eleven cities and towns with very heavy army stores.

JOHN H. MORGAN,
Colonel, Commanding Brigade.

If this report be true General Morgan will be compelled to de-tach a portion of his command. When he does so it will present the most favorable opportunity of pushing forward your operations, and probably enable you to enter Kentucky. The inclosed papers are forwarded for your information. The general directs that you return them after examination.

Lt. L. CLAY,
Assistant Adjutant-General.[4]

After observing Buell's army advancing toward Chattanooga, Bragg, partly to assist Kirby Smith, but mostly to protect the city from Union conquest, decided to move his troops there in advance of Buell.

Narrative of Kenneth Noe,
Perryville, This Grand Havoc of Battle

So it was that Kirby Smith's desperate appeal of the twenty-fourth [of July 1862] reached Bragg not in Tupelo, but rather in Montgom-ery, Alabama, with Bragg already riding the rails to the rescue. It was one of the boldest movements of the war. Starting on July 23 along the same circuitous, rickety, 776 mile-long path that McCown's division had traveled—which involved six separate railroads and a ferry ride across Mobile Bay—Bragg moved five thousand infan-trymen per day via Mobile and Montgomery to Chattanooga. The garrison Bragg had left at Mobile spearheaded the movement. Sup-ply wagons, cavalry, and artillery meanwhile started on overland roads across Alabama to Chattanooga via Rome, Georgia. The first of Bragg's units arrived in Chattanooga on July 27, with part of the army still in Tupelo waiting its turn. Within two weeks, the rickety Confederate railroad network incredibly had moved thirty-thousand infantrymen, and in so doing altered the direction of the war.[5]

Bragg and Kirby Smith finally met face-to-face on July 31 in Chattanooga. They agreed to conduct a joint campaign.

Message from Gen. Braxton Bragg to Gen. Samuel Cooper

HEADQUARTERS DEPARTMENT No. 2,
Chattanooga, Tenn, August 1, 1862.
S. COOPER, Adjutant and Inspector General:—

GENERAL: In pursuance of my purpose and plan of operations, reported from Tupelo, I reached here on the morning of the 30th ultimo. The troops are coming on as rapidly as the railways can carry them. Maj. Gen. E. Kirby Smith, commanding Department of East Tennessee, met me here yesterday by appointment, and we have arranged measures for mutual support and effective co-operation. As some ten days or two weeks must elapse before my means of transportation will reach here to such extent as to enable me to take the field with my main force it has been determined that General Smith shall move at once against General Morgan, in front of Cumberland Gap. Should he be successful, and our well-grounded hopes be fulfilled, our entire force will then be thrown into Middle Tennessee with the fairest prospect of cutting off General Buell, should that commander continue in his present position. Should he be re-enforced meantime from the west side of the Tennessee River, so as to cope with us, then Van Dorn and Price can strike and clear West Tennessee of any force that can be left to hold it. . . .

Respectfully, your obedient servant,
BRAXTON BRAGG
General, Commanding[6]

After all of Bragg's troops had finally arrived, he decided not to attempt to retake Nashville as Buell supposed he would. Rather, he advanced initially into Middle Tennessee and then Kentucky.

Report of Gen. Braxton Bragg, CSA,
Commanding Army of the Mississippi

Having crossed the river at Chattanooga the column took up its march on August 28 over Walden's Ridge and the Cumberland Mountains for Middle Tennessee. Major General Smith had already successfully passed through Northeastern Tennessee and gained the rear of Cumberland Gap, held by the enemy in strong force, well fortified. Leaving a sufficient force to hold the enemy in observation, his dislodgement being considered impracticable, he moved, as authorized, with the balance of his command on Lexington, Ky. This rich country, full of supplies so necessary to us, was represented to be occupied by a force which could make but feeble resistance. How well and successful that duty was performed has already been reported by General Smith. His complete victory over the enemy at Richmond, Ky., and his occupation of Lexington rendered it necessary for me to intercept General Buell, now moving rapidly toward Nashville, or to move toward the right, so as to secure a junction with General Smith when necessary.[7]

Unsure of both Bragg's and Kirby Smith's movements, Buell decided to retreat in order to protect Nashville and Louisville.

Message from Maj. Gen. Don Carlos Buell
to Maj. Gen. Henry Halleck

DECHARD, TENN, August 25, 1862,
Via Cairo, August 26, 1862, 3 p.m.

MAJ. GEN. H. W. HALLECK, General-in-Chief:

The want of cavalry in sufficient force for reconnaissance's in the extensive region through which the enemy may approach with mountain intervention to screen his movement makes us mainly dependent on spies and other sources for information in regard to his position until he is actually within reach. I have no doubt that I can concentrate my whole force in advance of this, my present information being that the enemy has not yet passed the Sequatchie Valley in force, although he is certainly on this side of the river. The difficulties of the last two months in keeping open our communications make it plain that no permanent advance into East Tennessee can be attempted without a much larger force than is at present under my command. While the enemy maintains his present attitude and strength every step in advance increases the demand for the main body to protect our lines. For the present no more can be attempted than to keep the enemy back by giving up some of our railroad lines. I hope to have a force about Nashville which will make the city secure against cavalry demonstration, reopen the road to Louisville, and still leave a concentrated force of about 30,000 men, but this force is altogether insufficient to render the State secure or exert much influence and control over the population. The necessity for removing troops from points heretofore occupied is to be much regretted. The whole country swarms with irregular cavalry or guerrillas, who keep down anything like exhibition of loyalty. I attach so much importance to the only foothold we have in Alabama that I have determined to hold on to Huntsville and the road from there to Stevenson even at the great risk to the small force I can possibly spare, trusting to early re-enforcements to make it more secure.

D. C. BUELL,
Major-General.[8]

The next stop on the tour entails a drive of about 181 miles to the Cumberland Gap. From 405 East Fifth Street, drive northwest, and immediately turn left (southwest) onto Georgia Avenue. Continue 3 blocks, and turn right (west) onto Seventh Avenue. Turn left (south) at the third cross street onto Market Street. Drive about 1.5 miles to the intersection with I-75. Take the I-75 East entrance lane onto I-75, and follow I-75 approximately 115 miles to Knoxville. From Knoxville, follow I-75 North to Exit 134, and go east on TN 63 about 38 miles to the intersection with US 25 East. Turn left (north) onto US 25 East, and continue 4.0 miles and take the Cumberland Gap National Historical Park exit. Follow the signs to the visitor center (606-248-2817; nps.gov/cuga).

This route somewhat follows the same path that Acting Brig. Gen. Preston Smith's and Brig. Gen. Patrick Cleburne's brigades traveled to Knoxville to reinforce Kirby Smith before he began his invasion of Kentucky. Past Knoxville, while driving east on TN 63, observe the mountains and gaps on your left (north). Parts of Kirby Smith's forces crossed into Kentucky through these formations.

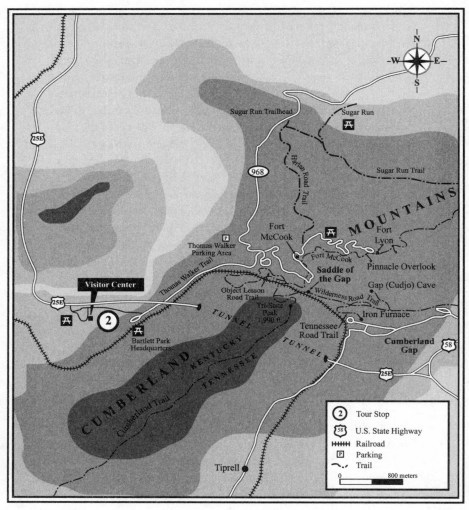

Driving Tour Stop 2,
Cumberland Gap, KY, TN, VA

You can get directions to the park's Civil War fortifications, once held by the Union's Brig. Gen. George W. Morgan. Other historic sites and view sites are available.

Stop 2—Cumberland Gap National Historic Park

Critical Decisions: (7) Kirby Smith Decides to Bypass Cumberland Gap and March to Lexington, (8) Kirby Smith Orders Morgan to Compromise Buell's Supply Line

Kirby Smith quickly realized that it would take much time to force the Union command holding Cumberland Gap to relinquish this crucial position. He also saw the glory that a successful invasion of Kentucky would potentially bring him and the Confederacy. Thus Kirby Smith decided to leave a part of his command to monitor the Union force at the gap and advance into Kentucky with the rest of his command.

Message from Maj. Gen. Edmund Kirby Smith to Gen. Braxton Bragg

HEADQUARTERS DEPARTMENT OF EAST TENNESSEE,
Barboursville, Ky., August 20, 1862.
General BRAXTON BRAGG,
Commanding Department No. 2, Chattanooga, Tenn.:

SIR: I arrived here with four brigades of infantry on the morning of the 18th instant. The small force of the enemy which had been encamped here retired on the evening of the 17th, taking the road to Cumberland Gap. We captured some 50 prisoners, including the sick (no supplies) and a few wagons. My information of the condition of affairs at the Gap is that [Union Brig. Gen. George W.] Morgan has supplies to last him from twenty to thirty days. By case mating the batteries and by making strong abatis in his front he has rendered his position (naturally strong), in my judgement, impregnable. The country around here having been almost completely drained of all kinds of supplies, and the roads between here and East Tennessee being much worse than I had supposed. I find I have but two courses left me—either to fall back for supplies to East Tennessee or to advance toward Lexington for them. The former course will be too disastrous to our cause in Kentucky for me to think of doing so for a moment. I have therefore decided to advance as soon as possible upon Lexington. If I do nothing more than get large quantities of supplies, which I can certainly do and then fall back here, I will be much better off than I am now; but I am not without hope that the move may be attended with brilliant results, as it will certainly give the Southern men of Kentucky an opportunity of rallying around the Confederate standard and I think must prove a most advantageous diversion for you in your movements against Buell. . . .

> I am, general, respectfully, your obedient servant,
> E. KIRBY SMITH,
> Major-General, Commanding.[9]

Meanwhile, Kirby Smith ordered Col. John H. Morgan and his cavalry to interdict Buell's supply line, the Louisville and Nashville Railroad. Morgan faithfully carried out those orders and temporarily destroyed the railroad tunnel at Gallatin, Tennessee. This severely hampered Buell's ability to receive necessary supplies.

Message to Gen. Braxton Bragg (*continued*)

I have ordered Colonel Morgan, after doing all the damage he can to the railroad between Nashville and Louisville, to push across the country and join me at Lexington, where I hope to be by September 2. I have also ordered Stevenson to send in an additional brigade, which will make my force nearly 10,000. . . .

> I am, general, respectfully, your obedient servant,
> E. KIRBY SMITH,
> Major-General, Commanding.[10]

Message from Maj. Gen. Edmund Kirby Smith
to President Jefferson Davis

HEADQUARTERS ARMY OF EAST TENNESSEE,
Barboursville, Ky., August 21, 1862.
His Excellency JEFFERSON DAVIS,
President of the Confederate States:

. . . . A report from Colonel Morgan also gives me the information that he has destroyed the tunnel on the railroad between Nashville and Louisville. I have therefore nothing to fear from Buell, and I will have opposed to me only the raw levies just being raised in the Northern States. Our presence will give the true men of Kentucky the opportunity for rallying to our standard, and in any event I can obtain large quantities of supplies, fall back here, and still be better off than now. . . .

> With high respect, I am, your obedient servant,
> **E. KIRBY SMITH,**
> Major-General, Commanding:[11]

The next stop requires an approximately 105-mile drive to reach the Richmond Battlefield Visitor Center. Leave the park, and rejoin US 25 East heading north. Drive about 46 miles to the intersection with I-75. Merge onto I-75 North, and drive to the Berea exit, which is Exit 76. Exit onto Chestnut Street, and follow it east about 1.5 miles to a slight right turn onto Prospect Street. Prospect Street becomes Big Hill Road. Drive about 5.0 miles to the intersection of US 421 South, also known as Battlefield Memorial Highway. Turn left (north) onto Battlefield Memorial Highway. Unless you are already familiar with the Battle of Richmond, continue 8.4 miles to the visitor center on the right, just before the merge with Berea Road. Park here, and obtain orientation at the visitor center (859-624-0013; battleofrichmond.org). You may then return south to find Phase One of the battle near the Mount Zion Church. You may consider each of these critical decisions while at the visitor center, or consider them if you follow the various phases of the battle.

Stop 3—Richmond, Kentucky Battlefield

Critical Decisions: (9) Nelson Splits His Forces Between Richmond and Lancaster, (10) Kirby Smith Decides to Attack the Union Force at Richmond, (12) Manson Moves South of Richmond to Defend the City, (13) Kirby Smith Orders Flank Attacks against Manson, (14) Kirby Smith Prepares to Capture Fleeing Union Troops

Maj. Gen. William "Bull" Nelson was in a quandary. He wanted to at once defend Kentucky from Kirby Smith's advance and carry out Buell's orders to protect the Louisville and Nashville Railroad. Thus Nelson split up his command, which consisted mostly of raw recruits. As a result, he was not initially present to defend either Richmond or Lexington.

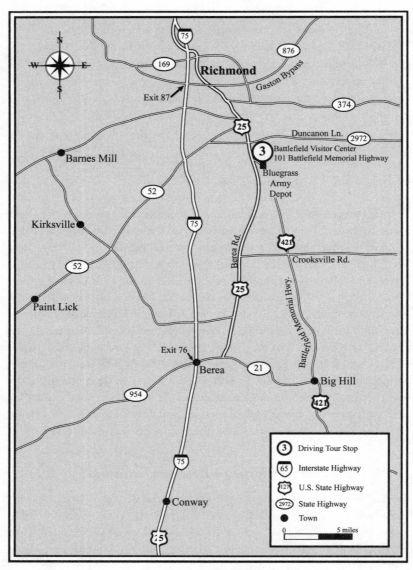

Driving Tour Stop 3,
Richmond Battlefield, KY

Message from Maj. Gen. William Nelson to
Maj. Gen. Horatio G. Wright

HEADQUARTERS ARMY OF KENTUCKY,
Richmond, August 27, 1862.
Maj. Gen. HORATIO G. WRIGHT,
Commanding Department of the Ohio:
GENERAL:
. . . . I shall establish the two brigades here in camp on Paint Creek, half-way between this and Lancaster. . . .
Permit me to remind you that the cutting of the railroad from Bowling Green to Nashville isolates Buell's army and leaves it without supplies. General Buell's directions to me were to open that road the first thing.

Very respectfully,
W. NELSON,
Major General, Commanding.[12]

As Kirby Smith advanced into Kentucky, he made Lexington his initial target. However, he worried that the Union command would fortify a strong defensive line on the north bank of the Kentucky River. Kirby Smith and his men were not likely to overrun this position. When he discovered that Manson was actually marching south to defend Richmond, Kirby Smith seized the initiative.

Narrative of James Lee McDonough,
War in Kentucky: From Shiloh to Perryville

[The Union's Maj. Gen. Horatio G.] Wright was not the only general who understood the potential advantage at the Kentucky River. The Rebel commander appreciated the situation too. Probably Kirby Smith recognized it as much or more than the Union general, and he feared that the Yankees would retreat to the river. If they did, his invasion, to state it bluntly, would likely come to naught, for Kirby Smith would have no desirable options. His path into the heart of the rich Bluegrass, where he could find supplies and hoped to find recruits for his army, would effectively be blocked. To force a crossing of such a formidable barrier would cost Kirby Smith's small Confederate army too many casualties—assuming the effort could succeed at all, which would be highly doubtful. Probably even inexperienced Federal defenders could bring his advance to a halt at the Kentucky River.[13]

Having observed this situation, Manson at once proceeded to launch into the Rebels [south of Richmond]. Kirby Smith was greatly relieved when he learned that the Yankees evidently were preparing to stand and fight; in fact, he rushed to close with the Federals, perhaps fearful that they would have a change of mind and retreat.[14]

Report of Brig. Gen. Mahlon D. Manson, USA, Commanding First Brigade, Army of Kentucky.

At 2 o clock p.m. of the same day a messenger arrived and informed me that the cavalry, under command of Colonel Metcalfe and Lieutenant-Colonel Munday, and the infantry picket, under command of Lieutenant-Colonel Wolfe, were retreating as fast as possible to the camp, and that the enemy, to the number of 4,000 or 5,000, was pressing hard upon them. The only question for me now to determine was whether I should allow the enemy to attack me in my camp or whether I should advance and meet him. It did not take me a moment to decide which course to pursue, as all the hills 1½ miles south of me completely commanded my camp, and I did not think it my duty to allow the enemy to obtain possession of them without a struggle. I therefore ordered forward the First Brigade, consisting of the Sixteenth, Fifty-fifth, Sixty.ninth, and Seventy-first Indiana Regiments, and the artillery under command of Lieutenant Lanphere.[15]

Report of Maj. Gen. Edmund Kirby Smith, CSA, Commanding Army of Kentucky

Without waiting for Churchill's division Cleburne at once commenced the action, and when I arrived on the field at 7.30 o'clock the fire of artillery was brisk on both sides. As my force was almost too small to storm the position in front without a disastrous loss I sent General Churchill with one of his brigades to turn the enemy's right. While this move was being executed a bold and well-conducted attempt on the part of the enemy to turn Cleburne's right was admirably foiled by the firmness of Col. Preston Smiths brigade, who repulsed the enemy with great slaughter.[16]

Report of Col. John Scott, CSA, Commanding
Scott's Cavalry Brigade, Army of Kentucky

On the morning of the 30th, in obedience to your [Kirby Smith's] orders, I passed around to the west of Richmond and took possession of the roads leading to Lexington. The majority of my forces were posted on the Lexington road and one company on the Lancaster road; the remainder between the two roads. About 4 o'clock stragglers from the battlefield commenced passing into my lines and gradually increased in numbers until 6 o'clock, when the main body of the enemy, apparently about 5,000 strong, with nine pieces of artillery, came upon us. My forces, being well ambuscaded, poured a destructive fire into their ranks, killing about 60 and wounding a large number, the firing commenced in obedience to my orders on the extreme left, extending to the right, which was nearest Richmond after which almost the entire force immediately surrendered. Owing to the smallness of my force (about 850) I was unable to still guard the roads and remove all the prisoners to the rear, and consequently a large number escaped, wandering through the corn fields and woodlands, it being now too dark to distinguish them when a few paces distant. I am unable to state positively the number of prisoners taken by my command, owing to the fact that they were captured principally after dark, and during the same night were turned over to General Preston Smith, in obedience to your orders, but am confident they could not fall short of 3,500. I captured also nine pieces of artillery, a large number of small-arms, and wagons loaded with army supplies. Among the prisoners captured were Brigadier-General Manson and a number of field and staff officers.[17]

The next stop is the Old Capitol in Frankfort, about 63 miles away. After touring the battlefield, depart the visitor center, and drive 2.8 miles north on US 25 / Berea Road to the intersection with Duncannon Road. Turn left (west), and drive 3.5 miles to the intersection with I-75. Merge north toward Lexington. In about 40 miles, after merging onto I-64 and remaining on I-64 after the split with I-75, take Exit 65 off of I-64. Turn left (south) onto KY 341, and then immediately after crossing under I-64, turn right (northwest) onto US 421 / Leestown Road. Drive 8 miles to where US 421 becomes the East-West Connector. Continue 2.3 miles to MLK Boulevard. Turn right (north) onto MLK Boulevard, and drive 0.7 mile to East Main Street. Turn

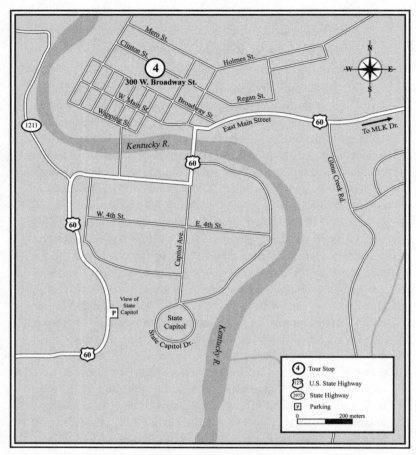

Driving Tour Stop 4,
Old Capitol Building, Frankfort, KY

left (west) onto East Main Street, and drive another 0.7 mile to East Broadway Street. Turn right (northwest) onto East Broadway, which will become West Broadway, drive 0.3 mile to the Old State Capitol on the right, and park. Visit the building if it is open (502-564-1792). Tickets are available at the Kentucky Historical Society, 100 West Broadway Street.

Stop 4—Old Kentucky State Capitol

Critical Decisions: (19) Bragg Unites with Kirby Smith and Assumes Command of Both Armies, (21) Bragg Installs a Confederate Governor at Frankfort.

After Bragg decided to leave Munfordville and unite with Kirby Smith, he marched his army to Lexington and joined with the junior officer's smaller force. Being far senior in rank, Bragg took command of Kirby Smith's men, a change that should have happened much earlier.

Report of Gen. Braxton Bragg, CSA, Commanding
Confederate Army of the Mississippi

On my arrival at Bardstown I learned from Major General Smith, then at Lexington, that the enemy was moving from Cumberland Gap, endeavoring to escape by the valley of Sandy River, in Eastern Kentucky, and that he had sent his whole force in pursuit. A sufficient force to prevent this escape and hold the enemy in check there and compel his surrender had been ordered and was confidently expected from another quarter to have followed General Smith's movement in time for this purpose. Circumstances unknown to me in our then isolated position, and over which I could not exercise control, had prevented this consummation so confidently relied on and so necessary to our success. The delay necessarily resulting from this pursuit of the enemy by General Smith prevented a junction of our forces, and enabled General Buell to reach Louisville before the assault could be made upon that city.

. . . I left Bardstown on the 28th for Lexington to confer with General Smith and inform myself fully as to our condition and the resources of the country.[18]

Then Bragg decided that the combined armies, rather than advancing against the invading Union army, would assist in the installation of a Confederate governor at the Kentucky Capitol at Frankfort. To Bragg's credit, this choice would allow him to formalize Confederate law within the state. He might then order conscription of local men to increase his rolls; there had been no draft thus far. By examining Bragg's communication below, it is obvious that he was less concerned with enemy movements and more concerned with inaugurating the Confederate governor.

Report of Gen. Braxton Bragg, CSA, Commanding
Confederate Army of the Mississippi

FRANKFORT, KENTUCKY., October 3, 1862-8 p.m.

[General POLK:]

DEAR GENERAL: I just have yours of yesterday p.m. I have sent you several dispatches since yesterday morning desiring you to move your force on the enemy, who was making a descent on this point. That move has proved to be only a feint and has ceased. You will act accordingly, but I desire you to hold your command ready for a junction at any moment, and if possible place one flank at Taylorsville. Just as soon as Morgan gets in from his pursuit of his namesake you shall have cavalry. To-morrow we inaugurate the civil Governor here, and transfer to him all that department. The brigades of Cleburne and Preston Smith will soon rejoin you. We have 5,000 men just arrived at Danville; 2,000 more I hear are nearly up, and Breckinridge has at last arrived at Knoxville, and [on] his way with his division. This will strengthen us. Recruiting is slow, but improving.

Yours, very truly,
BRAXTON BRAGG
General, Commanding.[19]

It is about 46 miles to the site of the next stop, Camp Dick Robinson. Drive ahead on West Broadway to the next intersection, which is Catfish Alley, and make a U-turn. Drive 3 blocks southeast on Broadway back to Ann Street. Turn right (southwest) onto Ann Street, and immediately merge into the left lane. In 1 block, turn left (east-southeast) onto Main Street. Drive east 0.9 mile to MLK Boulevard. Turn right (south) onto MLK Boulevard. and drive 0.7 mile, merging into the left lane. Turn left (east) onto the East-West Connector, and drive 1.9 miles to merge onto US 60 / Versailles Road. Continue south 9.7 miles to a slight right onto US 60 Business East. Continue 1.0 mile onto Main Street. After 1.1 miles, Main Street becomes KY 33. Follow KY 33 south 2.1 miles to a left turn (east) onto KY 169 South. In 7.0 miles, turn right (southwest) onto KY 1267 / KY 169 South. Drive 3 blocks, and turn left (southeast), remaining on KY 169 South / Keene Road. Continue 4.6 miles to the intersection with US 27 South. Turn right (southwest) onto US 27 South / Lexington Road, and continue 15.3 miles. Turn left (south), continuing to follow the Old Lexington Road. In 0.7 mile you will come to the intersection where Lexington Road turns southwest and meets the intersection of US 27 and KY 34. Continue straight past this right-hand turn about 0.1 mile to a pullout on the left and four interpretive markers describing Camp Dick Robinson. Park, read the markers, and observe the terrain to the east.

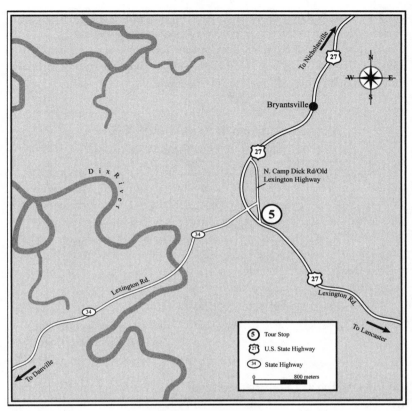

Driving Tour Stop 5,
Site of Camp Dick Robinson, KY

Stop 5—Camp Dick Robinson / Breckinridge

Critical Decisions: (26) Bragg Decides to Abandon Kentucky, (27) Buell Marches to Nashville, Allowing Bragg and Kirby Smith to Escape

As they continued advancing into central Kentucky, the Confederates concentrated supplies at the former Camp Dick Robinson, originally a Union recruiting and training camp established by Maj. Gen. William "Bull" Nelson. Rebels renamed the site Camp Breckinridge when they captured it, and Bragg regrouped his combined army there after the Battle of Perryville. Unfortunately, only a few days' worth of supplies remained. Here, Bragg informed his officers (and men) that he had decided to abandon Kentucky. While this decision was a practical one due to the lack of provisions, recruits, and water (drought), men in Bragg's army and throughout the Confederacy turned against him. His announcement marked the beginning of growing, festering animosity within his army, soon to be renamed the Army of Tennessee.

Report of Gen. Braxton Bragg, CSA, Commanding Army of the Mississippi

The campaign here was predicated on a belief and the most positive assurances that the people of this country would rise in mass to assert their independence. No people ever had so favorable an opportunity, but I am distressed to add there is little or no disposition to avail of it. Willing perhaps to accept their independence, they are neither disposed nor willing to risk their lives or their property in its achievement. With ample means to arm 20,000 men and a force with that to fully redeem the State we have not yet issued half the arms left us by casualties incident to the campaign.

I am, sir, very respectfully, your obedient servant,
BRAXTON BRAGG,[20]

Buell and the Lincoln administration confirmed that Bragg and Kirby Smith were retreating out of Kentucky via eastern Kentucky and Tennessee, and not a direct route to Nashville. Buell subsequently received orders to pursue and engage the Rebels before they could escape. However, he had no desire to do so, claiming that drought and lack of supplies made such a movement impractical. Buell redirected his army to Nashville, and he was quickly removed and replaced with Maj. Gen. William S. Rosecrans.

Message from Maj. Gen Don Carlos Buell to Maj. Gen. Henry W. Halleck

HEADQUARTERS ARMY OF THE OHIO,
October 16, 1862. (Received October 17.)

Major-General HALLECK, General-in-Chief:

You are aware that between Crab Orchard and Cumberland Gap the country is almost a desert. The limited supply of forage which the country affords is consumed by the enemy as he passes. In the day and a half that we have been in this sterile region our animals have suffered exceedingly. The enemy has been driven into the heart of this desert and must go on, for he cannot exist in it. For the same reason we cannot pursue in it with any hope of overtaking him, for while he is moving back on his supplies and as he goes consuming what the country affords we must bring ours forward. There is but one road and that a bad one. The route abounds in difficult defiles, in which a small force can retard the progress of a large one for a considerable time, and in that time the enemy could gain material advantage in a move upon other points. For these reasons, which I do not think it necessary to elaborate, I deem it useless and inexpedient to continue the pursuit, but propose to direct the main force under my command rapidly upon Nashville, which General Negley reported to me as already being invested by a considerable force and toward which I have no doubt Bragg will move the main part of his army. The railroads are being rapidly repaired and will soon be available for our supplies. In the mean time I shall throw myself on my wagon transportation, which, fortunately, is ample. While I shall proceed with these dispositions, deeming them to be proper for the public interest, it is but meant that I should say that the present time is perhaps as convenient as any for making any changes that may be thought proper in the command of this army. It has not accomplished all that I had hoped or all that faction might demand: yet, composed as it is, one-half of perfectly new troops, it has defeated a powerful and thoroughly disciplined army in one battle and has driven it away baffled and dispirited at least, and as much demoralized as an army can be under such discipline as Bragg maintains over all troops that he commands. I will telegraph you more in detail in regard to the disposition of troops in Kentucky and other matters to-morrow.

D. C. BUELL,
Major-General[21]

From Camp Dick Robinson it is only 18 miles to the Crawford House. Drive to the stoplight. Continue straight ahead on KY 34 4.7 miles to KY 2168. Turn left (south), and continue on KY 2168 / KY-34, which becomes Lexington Avenue. In about 2.0 miles, turn slightly right onto Lexington Avenue. Follow Lexington Avenue 0.9 mile to the intersection with Saint Mildred's Court. Turn left (south), drive 0.2 mile, and turn right (west) onto West Main Street. West Main becomes the Perryville Road / US 150. Drive about 9.5

miles to Perryville. US 150 becomes East Second Street. At the intersection with North Bragg Street, turn right (north) onto it. Continue 0.9 mile to the historic Crawford House on the left, and park. While part of the battlefield, the house is presently unsafe.

Stop 6—Crawford House / Perryville Battlefield

Critical Decisions: (22) Bragg Orders Polk to Attack a Union Corps at Perryville, (24) Bragg Realigns His Divisions and Attacks, (25) Bragg Retreats from Perryville

The Crawford House was Bragg's headquarters during the Battle of Perryville. Before the battle, he had ordered Lieut. Gen. Leonidas Polk to attack what was presumed to be only a part of Buell's army as it arrived at Perryville. Bragg remained convinced that the bulk of Buell's army was advancing farther north, and that the real battle for Kentucky would occur near Versailles. Polk feared a larger force was present and decided to maintain the offensive-defensive and take a wait-and-see attitude. Note that Bragg made the critical decision to order Polk and Hardee to halt the Union advance at Perryville before his arrival here.

Message from Gen. Braxton Bragg to Lieut. Gen. Leonidas Polk

HEADQUARTERS DEPARTMENT No. 2,
Harrodsburg, Ky., October 7, 1862, 5:40 p.m.

General Polk,

GENERAL: In view of the news from Hardee you had better move with Cheatham's division to his support and give the enemy battle immediately; rout him, and then move to our support at Versailles. Smith moves forward to-day in that direction, and I wish Withers to march to-night toward Lawrenceburg, crossing thence to-morrow to Versailles, and follow up Smith and report to him. His wagon train, except the ammunition and ordnance, had better cross at McCown's, turning off at Salvisa. No time should be lost in these movements. I shall follow Smith.

Respectfully and truly, yours,
BRAXTON BRAGG
General, Commanding.[22]

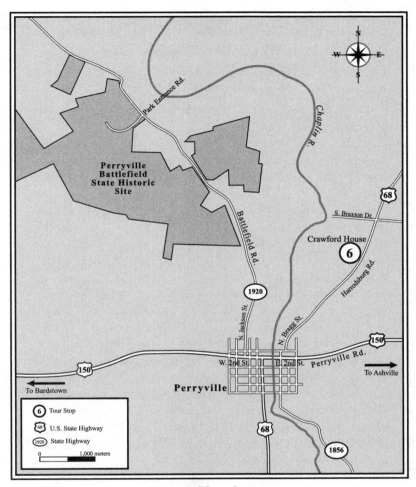

Driving Tour Stop 6,
Crawford House, Perryville, KY

The next morning, October 8, Bragg discerned an absence of gunfire from the Perryville area and rode there to investigate why his orders had apparently been disobeyed. Making his headquarters here at the Crawford House, he confronted Polk.

Report of Lieut. Gen. Leonidas Polk, CSA, Commanding Right Wing, Army of the Mississippi

HEADQUARTERS ARMY OF THE MISSISSIPPI
Knoxville, Tenn., November, 1862.

Sir: I have the honor to submit the following as my official report of the battle of Perryville:

. . . . Information having been received through General Hardee that the enemy was pressing with heavy force upon his position it was resolved by the general commanding the forces to attack him at that point. He accordingly directed me on the evening of the 7th to order Anderson's division of Hardees wing, to return to Perryville and also to order General Cheatham, with Donelson's division [brigade] of his wing, to follow it immediately, and to return myself to that place, to take charge of the forces and attack the enemy next morning. I urged the strong expediency of concentrating all our forces upon the point to be attacked, and at all events the necessity of having the remaining division of the Army of the Mississippi (Withers) placed at my disposal. To this the general objected, upon the ground that General Kirby Smith had informed him that the enemy was in force in his front and that his troops could not be spared from that part of the field, nor could the division of Withers be spared, as he thought the force in front of Smith made it necessary for him to be re-enforced. He therefore proposed to order Withers to the support of Smith and to take charge of those combined forces himself in person. Generals Anderson and Cheatham proceeded to Perryville and reported to General Hardee as ordered, and on arriving were posted by that officer in a line of battle which he had selected. I followed as soon as practicable, arrived during the night, and reconnoitered the line of battle early on the following morning.

At a meeting of the general officers, held about daylight, it was resolved, in view of the great disparity of our forces, to adopt the defensive-offensive, to await the movements of the enemy, and to be guided by events as they were developed. The line of battle selected was that indicated by the course of Chaplin Fork of Salt River, on the banks of which our troops were posted. The division of General Buckner, of the left wing, occupied the extreme right; that of General Anderson the center; that of General Donelson, of the right wing, under General Cheatham, the left. General Wharton's brigade of cavalry covered the right wing, General Wheeler the left. General

McCown, who reached the field by a forced march with a cavalry force at an early hour, was directed, by order of General Bragg, to turn over his command to Colonel Wheeler and to report to him for orders. The whole of our force, including all arms, did not exceed 15,000. We have good reason to believe that the force of General Buell immediately in front of us, consisting of the corps of Generals McCook and Gilbert, each about 18,000 strong, and that General Crittenden, with a corps of about the same, number, was within 8 miles of the field at the opening of the attack. General Liddell's brigade of General Buckner's division was thrown forward in observation about one mile in front of Perryville between the Springfield and Mackville roads. Light skirmishing opened the operation of the morning, which grew heavier as the day advanced. . . .

Respectfully, your obedient servant,
L. POLK,
Major-General, Commanding.[23]

Bragg was furious at the disobedience of his orders to attack. After viewing Polk's dispositions, Bragg quickly realized that a flank attack on his right might well counter a Rebel assault. He therefore realigned his command, ordering Cheatham's Division to march from the Rebel left to the far right and then attack.

Report of Gen. Braxton Bragg, CSA, Commanding Army of the Mississippi

Having ordered the attack and that no time should be lost, I was concerned at not hearing the commencement of the engagement early in the morning, but was much relieved for the time by receiving from General Polk a note, dated Perryville, 6 a. m. October 8, informing that the enemy's picketts commenced firing at daybreak and that he should bring on the engagement vigorously. . . . To my surprise, however, no gun was heard, and on my arrival, about 10 a. m., I was informed that is was determined not to attack but to assume the "defensive-offensive." After a hasty reconnaissance orders were given for some changes deemed necessary in the line of battle; a portion of it being withdrawn was restored, and Major General Polk was ordered to bring on the engagement. Impatient at the delay after this order I dispatched a staff officer to repeat it to the general, and soon thereafter I followed in person and put the troops in motion.[24]

After the fighting finally stopped after dark, Bragg, at the Crawford House, took stock of his situation. He became convinced that the Confederates' possession of the battlefield was in jeopardy, as was their ability to remain in Kentucky. Bragg subsequently held a meeting with his commanders and decided to retreat late that night.

Report of Gen. Braxton Bragg, CSA, Commanding Army of the Mississippi

The action, having at length commenced, was fought by our troops with a gallantry and persistent determination to conquer which the enemy could not resist; and though he was largely more than two to our one he was driven from the field with terrible loss. Night closed the operations just as a third corps of the enemy threw the head of its column against our left flank. We had entire possession of the battlefield, with thousands of the enemy's killed and wounded, several batteries of artillery, and 600 prisoners. For the details of this action, so creditable to our arms, I refer to the reports of subordinate commanders, herewith forwarded. In the progress of the engagement we had advanced so far as to expose our left flank to the third corps, just arrived from the direction of Lebanon. I therefore caused our line, which rested upon the field until midnight, to fall back to its original position. Assured that the enemy had concentrated his three corps against us, and finding that our loss had already been quite heavy in the unequal contest against two, I gave the orders to fall back at daylight on Harrodsburg, and sent instructions to Major-General Smith to move his command to form a junction with me at that place. There I again offered the enemy battle, which he declined. . . .

My whole force was accordingly retired on the 11th upon Bryantsville. Here the enemy again declined to advance upon me, but occupied himself in the destruction of the numerous mills and other sources from which we drew our only supply of breadstuffs.[25]

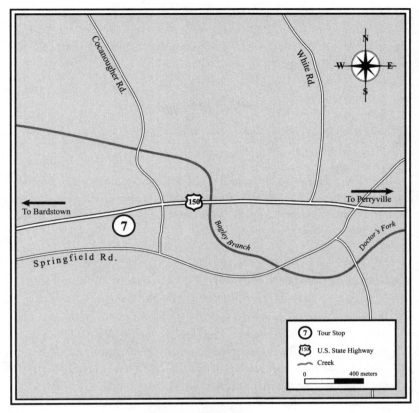

Driving Tour Stop 7,
Site of Buell's Headquarters, Perryville, KY

Return south on the Harrodsburg Road / North Bragg Street to the inter-section with East Second Street. Turn right (west) onto East Second Street. If you wish to visit the actual Perryville Battlefield, drive 4 blocks, crossing the Chaplin River, to Jackson Street. Turn right (north) onto Jackson Street, which becomes KY 1920 / Battlefield Road. Continue 2.1 miles to the en-trance to Perryville State Battlefield Site. Turn left, and proceed to the park headquarters / visitor center (859-332-8631; parks.ky.gov).

Return to downtown Perryville. From downtown Perryville the next stop is the site of Buell's headquarters. Drive west on US 150 about 2.6 miles to the intersection with the Old Springfield Road. Turn left (southwest) onto the Old Springfield Road, and follow it 1.0 mile to just past the intersection with Cocanougher Road. Pull over, and park on the right, where the road begins to curve to the southwest. Leave your vehicle, and look north. Do not trespass on private property.

Stop 7—Buell's Headquarters

Critical Decision: (23) Buell Delays the Attack on the Confederates at Perryville until October 9

The Dorsey House no longer exists, but it was located approximately halfway between the Old Springfield Road, which you are currently on, and the modern Highway 150 to the north. Note the short distance to the battlefield, yet Buell did not hear the ongoing battle.

Narrative of Kenneth Noe, *Perryville:* *This Grand Havoc of Battle*

With McCook late on the left and Crittenden even later on the right and out of touch most of the morning thanks to Thomas's borderline insubordination, Buell concluded between 10:30 and 11 A.M. that he could not strike the enemy at all that day with the overwhelming force his understanding of war demanded. Rear brigades would require all afternoon to come up. He thus made the momentous decision to postpone the attack until morning. The army would use the rest of the eighth to perfect its lines and hit Bragg the next day. In the meantime, the men could relax.[26]

The drive to the next stop, Bardstown, is about 32 miles. From the location of Buell's headquarters at the Dorsey House on October 8, drive 31.7 miles west on US 150 to the courthouse circle in downtown Bardstown. Park, and walk to the historical marker describing "Confederates Here" on the northwest corner of the circle.

Stop 8—Bardstown

Critical Decisions: (18) Buell Appoints "Maj. Gen." Charles Gilbert to Third Corps Command, (20) Buell Decides to Confront Bragg

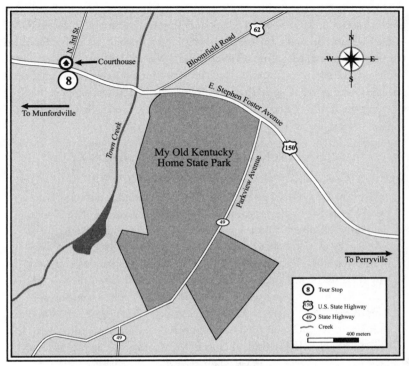

Driving Tour Stop 8,
Bardstown, KY

The Union Second and Third Corps passed through Bardstown on their way to Perryville. While Buell didn't make his two critical decisions in Bardstown, it is appropriate to discuss them here instead of driving all the way to Louisville, their actual site. Both Wheeler's and Wharton's cavalry brigades put up a strong but short-lived defense before being forced out of town. Bardstown then quickly changed sides, welcoming the Union troops as they arrived.

While in Louisville, Buell spent some time refitting and resupplying his men after their grueling retreat from the Nashville area. He also added new recruits to his army. In addition, Buell decided to once again maneuver against Bragg, fearing repercussions from Washington if he failed to do so. Yet Buell had been relieved of command and replaced by Thomas. However, Thomas did not want to replace Buell, who he felt had reorganized his army and should therefore be given a reasonable opportunity to command it while pursuing Bragg and Kirby Smith.

Once Buell had reorganized his army into three corps, he appointed Maj. Gens. Alexander McDowell McCook and Thomas I. Crittenden commanders of the First and Second Corps, respectively. Unfortunately, his choice for Third Corps commander, Maj. Gen. William "Bull" Nelson, had just been murdered by Brig. Gen. Jefferson C. Davis. Buell searched for a suitable replacement and selected "Acting Maj. Gen." Charles Gilbert, whose failure to support the First Corps at the Battle of Perryville cost Buell and the Union a victory there.

Narrative of Ezra J. Warner, *Generals in Blue: Lives of the Union Commanders*

After the Union disaster at the battle of Richmond, Kentucky, General Horatio G. Wright, commanding the Department of the Ohio, appointed Gilbert "acting major general" to command the Army of Kentucky after the wounding of General William Nelson; on September 4, 1862. Gilbert was appointed brigadier general of volunteers by the President. Until this time his career had been auspicious, his conduct uniformly praised by his superiors, and he had won the brevet of major for gallantry at Shiloh. But now the Army of the Ohio under D. C. Buell absorbed Gilbert's forces and he was named commander of the III Provisional Corps of that army. He led the corps at the battle of Perryville in October; even though he was subsequently brevetted lieutenant colonel for gallant and meritorious services, it appears that his direction of the corps left much to be desired. The Buell Commission[27] condemned him for failing to support Alex. McD. McCook's corps (on his left), which was driven back exposing Gilbert's own left flank; he was replaced and did not again hold field command.[28]

Report of Maj. Gen. Don Carlos Buell, USA, Commanding Army of the Ohio

These considerations determined me to concentrate rapidly at Louisville. The last division reached that point on the 29th of September. On the same day the incorporation of the new troops with the old, and other preparations which a long and fatiguing march of the old troops and the inefficiency of the new rendered necessary, were completed, and on the morning of the 30th the consolidated army was prepared to march against the rebel forces which occupied the principal part of Kentucky.[29]

Munfordville is about 55 miles away. Take the circle around and proceed west on Stephen Foster Avenue for 4 blocks. Turn left (southwest) onto US 31 East South / Cathedral Manor, drive 1.8 miles, and merge onto KY 9002 / Bluegrass Parkway. Continue on KY 9002 / Bluegrass Parkway 20 miles to merge onto I-65 South. Proceed south on I-65 to Exit 65, and exit. Turn left (southeast) on Main Street toward Munfordville. Drive 1.8 miles to the Hart County Historical Museum, and park. Visit the museum if it is open (270-524-0101; hartmuseum@scrtc.com). After your visit, continue southeast on Main Street / US 31 South / Dixie Highway for 1.3 miles, and turn right into the historical area parking lot, which is just past Richardson Road on the left. Park, and orient yourself. Follow the established trails if desired.

Stop 9—Munfordville

Critical Decisions: (16) Bragg Orders the Capture of the Garrison at Munfordville, (17) Bragg Decides Not to Fight Buell but to Join Kirby Smith

Once Bragg had his entire army transferred to Chattanooga, he marched into Middle Tennessee, decided to bypass Nashville, and advanced into Kentucky, eventually uniting with Kirby Smith to capture the state for the Confederacy. However, as Bragg marched north in Kentucky, he stumbled into a small confrontation that helped change his focus.

Kirby Smith sent his cavalry commander, Col. John Scott, to inform him of Bragg's and Buell's positions. Scott was also ordered to destroy any portions of the Louisville and Nashville Railroad to compromise Buell's supply line. As a result, Scott advanced to Munfordville, site of the longest bridge on the entire railroad. The eighteen-hundred-foot-long structure spanned the Green River at a height of over one hundred feet. Protected by a small detachment of Federal soldiers, Scott was surprised when this Union force refused to surrender to him. He contacted Brig. Gen. James Chalmers, whose men were already destroying parts of the railroad, and requested assistance in capturing the small Federal garrison at Munfordville.

Chalmers complied with Scott's request and attacked early on the morning of September 14. The result was a dismal failure. Bragg famously described this attack as "unauthorized and injudicious."[30] However, he decided to temporarily ignore Buell and capture this garrison in order to keep up the morale of his men, which he did. Bragg further decided to join up with Kirby Smith rather than engage Buell, allowing the Union army to escape back to Louisville. The message below covers both decisions.

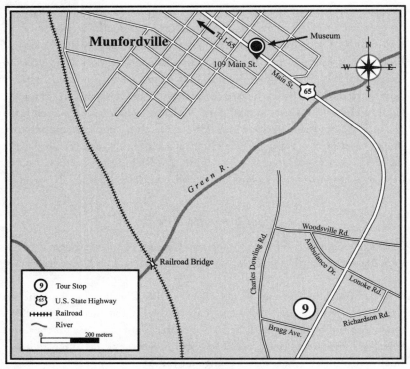

Driving Tour Stop 9,
Munfordville, KY

Message from Gen. Braxton Bragg to Gen. Samuel Cooper

General S. COOPER, Adjutant and Inspector General.
HEADQUARTERS DEPARTMENT No. 2,
Munfordville, Ky., September 17, 1862.

SIR: Since my last dispatch this army has moved on steadily in the accomplishment of its secondary object, a junction with Maj. Gen. E. K. Smith. Waiting two days in Glasgow to collect a supply of breadstuffs, an advance brigade thrown in this direction to cut the railroad and observe the enemy was indiscreetly advanced by its commander to the attack of a superior force here strongly fortified. After a most desperate fight they were repulsed with a loss of about 300 in killed and wounded. As soon as I heard of this misfortune my whole command was put in motion, and in less than twenty-four hours we had the place (some 25 and 35 miles distant by the routes taken) completely surrounded, and in a few hours an unconditional surrender of the whole garrison was made without our firing a gun. We received some 4,000 prisoners, an equal number of small-arms, 10 pieces of artillery, and munitions. The prisoners will be paroled and sent to General Buell at Bowling Green, the nearest point of the enemy's lines. My position must be exceedingly embarrassing to Buell and his army. They dare not attack me, and yet no other escape seems to be open to them.

My admiration of and love for my army cannot be expressed. To its patient toil and admirable discipline am I indebted for all the success which has attended this perilous undertaking. The men are much jaded and somewhat destitute, but cheerful and confident without a murmur.

We move soon on a combined expedition with General Smith.

Very respectfully, your obedient servant,
BRAXTON BRAGG,
General Commanding.[31]

The final stop on the driving tour features the railroad tunnels just north of Gallatin, TN, which were temporarily destroyed by Col. John H. Morgan during his raid into Kentucky. However, the tunnels are not accessible, nor is trespassing allowed on railroad property. Therefore, the stop will be at Goodlettsville, roughly twenty miles southwest of the actual location of the tunnels.

Goodlettsville is 89 miles south of Munfordville. Leave the parking area and turn right (southwest) onto US 31. Continue 1.1 miles and bear right onto KY 335. Continue 4.1 miles to the intersection with KY 218. Drive over I-65, and then turn left (south) on the entrance ramp to I-65 South. Follow I-65 South about 89 miles and take Exit 97. Turn left (west) onto Long Hollow Pike, and park where convenient.

Stop 10—Gallatin Tunnels

Critical Decision: (8) Kirby Smith Orders Morgan to Compromise Buell's Supply Line

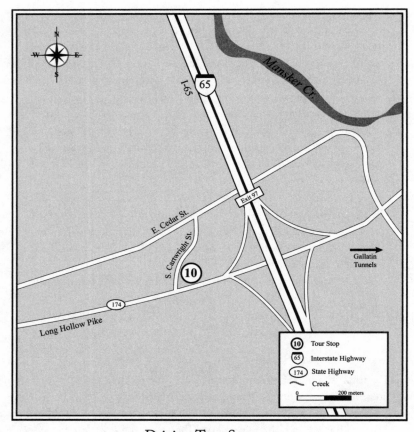

Driving Tour Stop 10,
Near Gallatin Tunnels, Goodlettsville, TN

Before Kirby Smith launched his own campaign into Kentucky, after pretending to agree to a joint campaign with Bragg, he had ordered Col. John H. Morgan to raid there. Specifically, Morgan was to damage Buell's supply line, the Louisville and Nashville Railroad. Morgan spectacularly obeyed his orders when he temporarily destroyed the tunnel about eight miles north of Gallatin, Tennessee, along with bridges. This damage severely curtailed Buell's ability to receive supplies; all provisions loaded on the railroad cars had to be unloaded, carried around the tunnel, reloaded on railroad cars south of the tunnel, and carried south. Buell was forced to retreat to Louisville to better reconnect with his supply line there. Thus Morgan's feat significantly altered Buell's plans.

Report of Maj. Gen. George Buell, USA, Commanding Army of the Ohio

In the meantime the enemy continued his operations with large bodies of cavalry against our long lines of communication through Tennessee and Kentucky, seconded in Tennessee by the organization of guerrilla bands, which swarmed in every part of the country. These latter were frequently encountered and defeated by detachments of our small cavalry force; but the former, moving in superior force and striking at vulnerable points, were generally successful, and finally on the 10th of August severed effectually our communications between Nashville and Louisville. In addition to the destruction of our lines of communication the effect of these operations and of the formidable preparations which were reported and believed to be in progress for the invasion of Middle Tennessee and the capture of Nashville was to intimidate our friends and embolden our enemies among the people, who not only would not bring in supplies voluntarily, but used every means to prevent us from finding them, so that nothing could be obtained from the country except by means of our own trains under the protection of strong escorts. On the 6th of August I gave orders for fortifying Nashville, to make it secure with a small garrison against any attack from cavalry. On the 10th of August Morgan again made his appearance at Gallatin, surprised and captured the garrison, amounting to 150 infantry; then moved toward Nashville, destroying several bridges and capturing the guards; then toward Bowling Green, destroying the tunnel 7 miles north of Gallatin and several trestle-works and small bridges in that region. He was, however, handsomely repulsed in some instances by the small force opposed to him in these attacks. Simultaneously with this Forrest, with a large force, moved toward the Cumberland River, to be in a position to support Morgan or threaten Nashville if it should diminish its garrison, which consisted of about 2,000 men. Immediately after the occurrence of the first raid I determined to withdraw my cavalry as much as possible from its service in detachments against the bands of guerrillas which infested the roads and concentrate it in large bodies. By supporting them with infantry, equipped to move lightly, I hoped to be able to drive the enemy's heavy cavalry force from the lines. One of these commands I designed should operate from Murfreesborough [*sic*] and another from McMinnville.[32]

Chattanooga is about 144 miles away. Return to I-65 South. Follow I-65 South about 11 miles, and merge onto I-24 South. Follow I-24 South through Nashville and back to Chattanooga, or exit where appropriate for you. This concludes the driving tour.

APPENDIX II

UNION ORDER OF BATTLE

Battle of Richmond, Kentucky
August 30, 1862

PROVISIONAL ARMY OF KENTUCKY
Maj. Gen. William Nelson

ESCORT
Ninth Kentucky Cavalry (2 Companies)

FIRST BRIGADE
Brig. Gen. Mahlon D. Manson
16th Indiana, Col. Thomas Lucas
55th Indiana, Lieut. Col. John R. Mahan
69th Indiana, Lieut. Col. Herman J. Korff
71st Indiana, Lieut. Col. Melville D. Topping
Battery F, Battery G, 1st Michigan (Improvised)
Light Artillery, Lieut. Edwin O. Lamphere

SECOND BRIGADE
Brig. Gen. Charles Cruft
12th Indiana, Col. William Link
66th Indiana, Maj. Thomas G. Morrison
18th Kentucky, Col. William A. Warner

95th Ohio, Col. William L. McMillen
Battery F, 1st Michigan Light Artillery (1 section), Lieut. Luther F. Hale

UNATTACHED, UNDER CRUFT
7th Kentucky (8 companies), Capt. Elisha B. Treadway
3rd Tennessee (2 companies?), Lieut. Col. John C. Chiles

CAVALRY BRIGADE
Brig. Gen. James Jackson
7th Kentucky Cavalry, Col. Leonidas Metcalfe
9th Pennsylvania Cavalry (2 battalions), Col. Edward C. Williams
6th Kentucky Cavalry (4 companies), Lieut. Col. Ruben Munday
9th Kentucky Cavalry, Col. Richard Jacob

Battle of Perryville, Kentucky
October 8, 1862

ARMY OF THE OHIO
Maj. Gen. Don Carlos Buell

ESCORT
Anderson's Troop, Pennsylvania Cavalry, Lieut. Thomas S. Maple
4th US Cavalry (6 companies), Lieut. Col. James Oakes

FIRST CORPS
Maj. Gen. Alexander McDowell McCook

THIRD DIVISION
Brig. Gen. Lovell H. Rousseau

NINTH BRIGADE
Col. Leonard A. Harris
38th Indiana, Col. Benjamin F. Scribner
2nd Ohio, Lieut. Col. John Kell
33rd Ohio, Lieut. Col. Oscar F. Moore
94th Ohio, Col. Joseph W. Frizell
10th Wisconsin, Col. Alfred R. Chapin
5th Indiana Light Artillery, Capt. Peter Simonson

SEVENTEENTH BRIGADE
Col. William H. Lytle

42nd Indiana, Col. James G. Jones
88th Indiana, Col. George Humphrey
15th Kentucky, Col. Curran Pope
3rd Ohio, Col. John Beatty
10th Ohio, Lieut. Col. Joseph Burke
1st Battery, Michigan Light Artillery, Capt. Cyrus O. Loomis

TWENTY-EIGHTH BRIGADE
Col. John C. Starkweather
24th Illinois, Capt. August Mauff
79th Pennsylvania , Col. Henry A. Hambright
1st Wisconsin, Lieut. Col. George B. Bingham
21st Wisconsin, Col. Benjamin Sweet
4th Battery, Indiana Light Artillery, Capt. Asahel K. Bush
Battery A, Kentucky Light Artillery, Capt. David C. Stone

UNATTACHED
2nd Kentucky Cavalry (6 companies), Col. Buckner Board
1st Michigan Engineers and Mechanics (3 companies),
Maj. Enos Hopkins

TENTH DIVISION
Brig. Gen. James S. Jackson

THIRTY-THIRD BRIGADE
Brig. Gen. William R. Terrill
Garrard's Detachment (3 companies), Col. Theophilius T. Garrard
80th Illinois, Col. Thomas G. Allen
123rd Illinois, Col. James Monroe
105th Ohio, Col. Albert S. Hall
Parson's (Improvised) Battery, Lieut. Charles C. Parson

THIRTY-FOURTH BRIGADE
Col. George Webster
80th Indiana, Col. Jonah R. Taylor
50th Ohio, Lieut. Col. Silas Strickland
98th Ohio, Lieut. Col. Christian Poorman
121st Ohio, Col. William P. Reid
19th Battery, Indiana Light Artillery, Capt. Samuel J. Harris

SECOND CORPS
Maj. Gen. Thomas L. Crittenden

FOURTH DIVISION
Brig. Gen. William Sooy Smith

TENTH BRIGADE
    Col. William Grose
    84th Illinois, Col. Louis H. Waters
    36th Indiana, Lieut. Col. Oliver H. P. Cary
    23rd Kentucky, Lieut. Col. J. P. Jackson
    6th Ohio, Col. N. L. Anderson
    24th Ohio, Lieut. Col. Frederick C. Jones
    Battery H, 4th US Artillery, Lieut. S. Canby
    Battery M, 4th US Artillery (2 sections), Capt. John Mendenhall

NINETEENTH BRIGADE
    Col. William B. Hazen
    110th Illinois, Col. Thomas S. Casey
    9th Indiana, Col. William H. Blake
    6th Kentucky, Col. Walter C. Whitaker
    27th Kentucky, Col. C. D. Pennebaker
    41st Ohio, Lieut. Col. George S. Mygatt
    Battery F, 1st Ohio Light Artillery, Capt. Daniel T. Cockerill

TWENTY-SECOND BRIGADE
    Brig. Gen. Charles Cruft
    31st Indiana, Lieut. Col. John Osborn
    1st Kentucky, Lieut. Col. David A. Enyart
    2nd Kentucky, Col. Thomas D. Sedgewick
    20th Kentucky, Lieut. Col. Charles S. Hanson
    90th Ohio, Col. Isaac N. Rose
    Battery B, 1st Ohio Light Artillery, Capt. William E. Standart

CAVALRY
    2nd Kentucky Cavalry (4 companies), Lieut. Col. Thomas Cochran

FIFTH DIVISION
Brig. Gen. Horatio P. Van Cleve

ELEVENTH BRIGADE
    Col. Samuel Beatty
    79th Indiana, Col. Frederick Knefler
    9th Kentucky, Lieut. Col. George Cram
    13th Kentucky, Lieut. Col. J. B. Carlile

19th Ohio, Lieut. Col. E. W. Hollingsworth
59th Ohio, Col. James P. Fyffe
7th Battery, Indiana Light Artillery, Capt. George Swallow

FOURTEENTH BRIGADE
Col. Pierce B. Hawkins
44th Indiana, Col. Hugh B. Reed
86th Indiana, Col. Orville S. Hamilton
11th Kentucky, Lieut. Col. S. P. Love
26th Kentucky, Col. Cicero Maxwell
13th Ohio, Col. Joseph C. Hawkins
Battery B, 26th Pennsylvania Light Artillery, Lieut. Alanson Stevens

TWENTY-THIRD BRIGADE
Col. Stanley Matthews
35th Indiana, Col. Bernard Mullen
8th Kentucky, Col. Sidney Barnes
21st Kentucky, Col. Samuel W. Price
51st Ohio, Lieut. Col. Richard McClain
99th Ohio, Lieut. Col. John E. Cummins
3rd Battery, Wisconsin Light Artillery, Capt. Lucius Drury

SIXTH DIVISION
Brig. Gen. Thomas J. Wood

FIFTEENTH BRIGADE
Brig. Gen. Milo S. Hascall
100th Illinois, Col. Frederick Bartleson
17th Indiana, Lieut. Col. George W. Gorman
58th Indiana, Col. George P. Buell
3rd Kentucky, Lieut. Col. William Scott
26th Ohio, Maj. Chris Degenfeld
8th Battery, Indiana Light Artillery, Lieut. George Estep

TWENTIETH BRIGADE
Col. Charles G. Harker
51st Indiana, Col. Abel D. Streight
73rd Indiana, Col. Gilbert Hathaway
13th Michigan, Lieut. Col. F. W. Gordon
64th Ohio, Col. John Ferguson
65th Ohio, Lieut. Col. William Young
6th Battery, Ohio Light Artillery, Capt. Cullen Bradley

TWENTY-FIRST BRIGADE
    Col. George D. Wagner
    15th Indiana, Lieut. Col. Gustavus Wood
    40th Indiana, Col. John Blake
    57th Indiana, Col. Cyrus Hines
    24th Kentucky, Col. Lewis B. Grigsby
    97th Ohio, Col. John Lane
    10th Battery, Indiana Light Artillery, Capt. Jerome B. Cox

FIRST CAVALRY BRIGADE
    Col. Edward D. McCook
    2nd Indiana Cavalry, Lieut. Col. Robert Stewart
    1st Kentucky Cavalry, Col. Frank Wolford
    3rd Kentucky Cavalry, Col. Eli Murray
    7th Pennsylvania Cavalry (1st Battalion), Maj. John E. Wynkoop
    Battery M, 4th US Light Artillery (1 section), Lieut. Henry A.
        Huntington

UNATTACHED
    1st Michigan Engineers and Mechanics (4 companies),
        Col. William Innes
    1st Ohio Cavalry (4 companies), Maj. James Laughlin
    3rd Ohio Cavalry (4 companies), Maj. John H. Foster

THIRD CORPS
(Acting) Maj. Gen. Charles C. Gilbert

FIRST DIVISION
    Brig. Gen. Albin Schoepf

FIRST BRIGADE
    Col. Moses B. Walker
    82nd Indiana, Col. Morton Hunter
    12th Kentucky, Col. William Hoskins
    17th Ohio, Col. John Connell
    31st Ohio, Lieut. Col. Frederick Lister
    38th Ohio, Lieut. Col. William Choate
    Battery D, 1st Michigan Light Artillery, Capt. J. W. Church

SECOND BRIGADE
    Brig. Gen. Speed S. Fry

    10th Indiana, Col. William Kise
    74th Indiana, Col. Charles W. Chapman
    4th Kentucky, Col. John Croxton
    10th Kentucky, Lieut. Col. William Hayes
    14th Ohio, Lieut. Col. George Este
    Battery C, 1st Ohio Light Artillery, Capt. D. K. Southwick

THIRD BRIGADE
    Brig. Gen. James B. Steedman
    87th Indiana, Col. Kline G. Shyrock
    2nd Minnesota, Col. James George
    9th Ohio, Lieut. Col. Charles Joseph
    35th Ohio, Col. Ferdinand Van Derveer
    18th US, Maj. Frederick Townsend
    Battery I, 4th US Light Artillery, Lieut. Frank G. Smith

UNATTACHED
    1st Ohio Cavalry (6 companies), Col. Minor Milliken

NINTH DIVISION
    Brig. Gen. Robert D. Mitchell

THIRTEENTH BRIGADE
    Col. Michael Gooding
    59th Illinois, Maj. Joshua C. Winters
    74th Illinois, Col. James B. Kerr
    75th Illinois, Lieut. Col. John E. Bennett
    22nd Indiana, Lieut. Col. Squire I. Keith
    5th Battery, Wisconsin Light Artillery, Capt. Oscar F. Pinney

THIRTY-FIRST BRIGADE
    Col. William P. Carlin
    21st Illinois, Col. John Alexander
    38th Illinois, Maj. Daniel Gilmer
    101st Ohio, Col. Leander Stem
    15th Wisconsin, Col. Hans C. Heg
    2nd Minnesota, Battery (2 sections), Lieut. Richard L. Dawley

THIRTY-SECOND BRIGADE
    Col. William W. Caldwell
    25th Illinois, Lieut. Col. James McClelland
    35th Illinois, Lieut. Col. William Chandler

81st Indiana, Lieut. Col. John Timberlake
8th Kansas Battalion, Lieut. Col. John Martin
8th Battery, Wisconsin Light Artillery, Capt. Stephen J. Carpenter

CAVALRY
36th Illinois (1 company), Capt. Samuel B. Sherer

ELEVENTH DIVISION
Brig. Gen. Philip H. Sheridan

THIRTY-FIFTH BRIGADE
Lieut. Col. Bernard Laiboldt
44th Illinois, Capt. Wallace W. Barrett
73rd Illinois, Col. James F. Jaques
2nd Missouri, Capt. Walter Hoppe
15th Missouri, Maj. John Weber

THIRTY-SIXTH BRIGADE
Col. Daniel McCook
85th Illinois, Col. Robert S. Moore
86th Illinois, Col. David D. Irons
125th Illinois, Col. Oscar Harmon
52nd Ohio, Lieut. Col. Daniel D. T. Cowen

THIRTY-SEVENTH BRIGADE
Col. Nicholas Greusel
36th Illinois, Capt. Silas Miller
88th Illinois, Col. Francis T. Sherman
21st Michigan, Col. Ambrose Stevens
24th Wisconsin, Col. Charles H. Larrabee

ARTILLERY
Battery I, Illinois Light Artillery, Capt. Charles M. Barnett
Battery G, 1st Missouri Light Artillery, Capt. Henry Hescock

THIRD CAVALRY BRIGADE
(Acting Brig. Gen.) Ebenezer Gay
9th Kentucky Cavalry (8 companies), Lieut. Col. John Boyle
2nd Michigan Cavalry, Lieut. Col. Archibald Campbell
9th Pennsylvania Cavalry, Lieut. Col. Thomas James
2nd Battery, Minnesota Light Artillery (1 section),
    Capt. William A. Hotchkiss

APPENDIX III

CONFEDERATE ORDER OF BATTLE

Battle of Richmond, Kentucky
August 30, 1862

CONFEDERATE ARMY OF KENTUCKY
Maj. Gen. Edmund Kirby Smith

ESCORT
1st Florida Cavalry (3 companies), Capt. William Footman
Nelson Rangers, Capt. T. H. Nelson

STEVENSON'S DIVISION (FIRST DIVISION)
Not present for the battle

HETH'S DIVISION (SECOND DIVISION)
Not present for the battle

CHURCHILL'S DIVISION (THIRD DIVISION)
Brig. Gen. Thomas J. Churchill

McCRAY'S BRIGADE (FIRST BRIGADE)
Col. Thomas H. McCray

10th Texas Dismounted Cavalry, Col. C. R. Earp
11th Texas Dismounted Cavalry, Col. John C. Burks
14th Texas Dismounted Cavalry, Col. Matthew D. Ector
32nd Texas Dismounted Cavalry, Lieut. Col. James Weaver
McCray's Arkansas Sharpshooters, Maj. James W. Clark

McNair's Brigade (Second Brigade)
   Col. Evander McNair
   1st Arkansas Dismounted Rifles, Col. Daniel H. Reynolds
   2nd Arkansas Dismounted Rifles, Col. Harris Flanagin
   4th Arkansas, Lieut. Col. Henry C. Bunn
   4th Arkansas Battalion, Maj. J. A. Ross
   30th Arkansas, Col. Charles J. Turnbull
   Humphrey's Arkansas Battery, Capt. John T. Humphrey

Cleburne's Division (Fourth Division)
   Brig. Gen. Patrick R. Cleburne
   (Acting) Brig. Gen. Preston Smith

Smith's Brigade (First Brigade)
   (Acting) Brig. Gen. Preston Smith
   Col. Alfred J. Vaughan Jr.
   12th Tennessee, Col. Tyree H. Bell
   13th Tennessee, Col. Alfred J. Vaughan Jr.
   47th Tennessee, Lieut. Col. W. E. Holmes
   154th (Senior) Tennessee, Col. Edward Fitzgerald
   Marion's Florida Light Artillery, Capt. John M. Martin

Hill's Brigade (Second Brigade)
   Col. Benjamin J. Hill
   13th/15th Consolidated Arkansas, Col. Lucius E. Polk
   2nd Tennessee, Lieut. Col. John A. Butler
   5th Tennessee, Lieut. Col. Joseph A. Smith
   48th Tennessee, Col. George H. Nixon
   1st Texas Artillery Battery, Capt. James P. Douglas

(Independent) Cavalry Brigade
   Col. John Scott
   1st Georgia Cavalry, Col. James J. Morrison
   1st Louisiana Cavalry, Lieut. Col. James O. Nixon
   4th Tennessee Cavalry, Col. James Starnes
   Buckner Guards, Capt. William L. Garriott
   Mountain Howitzer Battery, Lieut. William H. Holmes

SECOND KENTUCKY CAVALRY, COL. JOHN H. MORGAN
Not present for the battle

Battle of Perryville, Tennessee
October 8, 1862

CONFEDERATE ARMY OF THE MISSISSIPPI
Gen. Braxton Bragg

ESCORT
3rd Tennessee Cavalry (4 companies), Capt. W. C. Bacot
13th Tennessee Cavalry Battalion (Company I),
Capt. William W. Lilliard

RIGHT WING
Maj. Gen. Leonidas Polk

CHEATHAM'S DIVISION
Maj. Gen. Benjamin F. Cheatham

DONELSON'S BRIGADE
Brig. Gen. Daniel S. Donelson
8th Tennessee, Col. William L. Moore
15th Tennessee, Col. Robert C. Tyler
16th Tennessee, Col. John H. Savage
18th Tennessee, Col. John C. Carter
51st Tennessee, Col. John Chester
Carnes's Tennessee Battery, Capt. William W. Carnes

STEWART'S BRIGADE
Brig. Gen. Alexander P. Stewart
4th Tennessee, Col. Otho F. Strahl
5th Tennessee, Col. Calvin D. Venable
24th Tennessee, Lieut. Col. Hugh L. W. Bratton
31st Tennessee, Col. Egbert E. Tansil
33rd Tennessee, Col. Warner P. Jones
Stanford's Mississippi Battery, Capt. Thomas J. Stanford

MANEY'S BRIGADE
Brig. Gen. George Maney
41st Georgia, Col. Charles A. McDaniel
1st Tennessee, Col. Hume R. Feild

6th Tennessee, Col. George C. Porter
9th Tennessee, Lieut. Col. John W. Buford
27th Tennessee, Lieut. Col. William Frierson
Smith's Mississippi Battery, Lieut. William B. Turner

SMITH'S BRIGADE
Brig. Gen. Preston Smith
12th Tennessee, Col. Tyree H. Bell
13th Tennessee, Col. Alfred J. Vaughan Jr.
47th Tennessee, Col. Munson R. Hill
154th Senior Tennessee, Col. Michael Magevney Jr.
9th Texas, Col. William H. Young
Scott's Tennessee Battery, Capt. William L. Scott

WHARTON'S CAVALRY BRIGADE
Col. John A. Wharton
2nd Georgia Cavalry (5 companies), Lieut. Col. Arthur Hood
1st Kentucky Cavalry, (4 companies), Capt. Thomas A. Ireland
4th Tennessee Cavalry, (5 companies), Maj. Baxter Smith
Davis's Tennessee Cavalry Battalion (4 companies), Maj. John Davis
8th Texas Cavalry, Lieut. Col. Thomas Harrison

LEFT WING
Maj. Gen. William J. Hardee

ANDERSON'S DIVISION
Brig. Gen. J. Patton Anderson

BROWN'S BRIGADE
Brig. Gen. John C. Brown
1st Florida, Col. William Miller
3rd Florida, Col. Daniel B. Bird
41st Mississippi, Col. William F. Tucker
Battery A, 14th Battalion, Georgia Light Artillery,
    Capt. Joseph E. Palmer

ADAMS'S BRIGADE
Brig. Gen. Daniel W. Adams
13th Louisiana, Col. Randall L. Gibson
14th Battalion, Louisiana Sharpshooters, Maj. John E. Austin
16th Louisiana, Col. Daniel C. Gober
20th Louisiana, Col. August Reichard

25th Louisiana, Col. Stewart W. Fisk
5th Company, Washington Artillery, Capt. Cuthbert H. Slocomb

POWELL'S BRIGADE
Col. Samuel Powell
45th Alabama, Col. James G. Gilchrist
1st Arkansas, Col. John W. Colquitt
24th Mississippi, Col. William F. Dowd
29th Tennessee, Lieut. Col. Horace Rice
Barret's Missouri Battery, Capt. Overton W. Barret

JONES'S BRIGADE
Col. Thomas M. Jones
27th Mississippi, Lieut. Col. James L. Autry
30th Mississippi, Col. George G. F. Neill
34th Mississippi, Col. Samuel Benton
Battery F, 2nd Alabama Light Artillery, Capt. Charles L. Lumsden

BUCKNER'S DIVISION
Maj. Gen. Simon B. Buckner

LIDDELL'S BRIGADE
Brig. Gen. St. John R. Liddell
2nd Arkansas, Col. John Gratiot
5th Arkansas, Col. Lucius P. Featherston
6th Arkansas, Col. Alexander T. Hawthorn
7th Arkansas, Col. D. A. Gillespie
8th Arkansas, Col. John H. Kelly
Swett's Mississippi Battery, Lieut. Thomas Havern

CLEBURNE'S BRIGADE
Brig. Gen. Patrick R. Cleburne
13th/15th Arkansas, Col. Lucius E. Polk
2nd Tennessee, Capt. C. P. Moore
35th Tennessee, Col. Benjamin J. Hill
48th Tennessee, Col. George H. Nixon
Key's Section, Calvert's Arkansas Battery, Lieut. Thomas J. Key

JOHNSON'S BRIGADE
Brig. Gen. Bushrod R. Johnson
5th Confederate, Col. James A. Smith
17th Tennessee, Col. Albert S. Marks
23rd Tennessee, Lieut. Col. Richard H. Keeble

25th Tennessee, Col. John M. Hughes
37th Tennessee, Col. Moses White
44th Tennessee, Col. John S. Fulton
Darden's Mississippi Battery, Capt. Putnam Darden

WOOD'S BRIGADE

Brig. Gen. Sterling A. M. Wood
16th Alabama, Col. William B. Wood
33rd Alabama, Col. Samuel Adams
3rd Confederate, Lieut. Col. Henry V. Keep
3rd Georgia Cavalry (2 companies), Capt. Reuben L. Hill
15th Battalion Mississippi Sharpshooters, Maj. A. T. Hawkins
32nd Mississippi, Col. Mark P. Lowrey
45th Mississippi, Col. Aaron B. Hardcastle
Semple's Alabama Battery, Capt. Henry C. Semple

WHEELER'S CAVALRY BRIGADE

Col. Joseph Wheeler
1st Alabama Cavalry, Col. William W. Allen
3rd Alabama Cavalry, Col. James Hagan
6th Confederate Cavalry, Lieut. Col. James Pell
8th Confederate Cavalry, Col. W. B. Wade
2nd Georgia Cavalry Battalion, Maj. C. A. Whaley
Smith's Georgia Cavalry Battalion, Col. John R. Hart
1st Kentucky Cavalry (5 companies), Maj. John W. Caldwell
6th Kentucky Cavalry (3 companies), Col. J. Warren Grigsby
9th Tennessee Cavalry, Lieut. James D. Bennett
12th Tennessee Cavalry Battalion (4 companies),
    Lieut. Col. T. W. Adrian
Hanley's Section, Calvert's Arkansas Battery, Lieut. S. G. Hanley

NOTES

Preface

1. Lawrence K. Peterson, *Confederate Combat Commander: The Remarkable Life of Brigadier General Alfred Jefferson Vaughan Jr.* (Knoxville: University of Tennessee Press, 2013).

2. Ibid., 43–98.

Introduction

1. Roy P. Basler, ed., *The Collected Works of Abraham Lincoln, 9 vols.* (New Brunswick, NJ, Rutgers University Press, 1953-55), 4:532.

Chapter 1. Before the Campaign, June 9–July 31, 1862

1. Thomas Lawrence Connelly, *Army of the Heartland: The Army of Tennessee, 1861–1862* (Baton Rouge: Louisiana State University Press, 1967), 178.

2. James Lee McDonough, *War in Kentucky: From Shiloh to Perryville* (Knoxville: University of Tennessee Press, 1994), 20–22.

3. John E. Clark Jr., *Railroads in the Civil War: The Impact of Management on Victory and Defeat* (Baton Rouge: Louisiana State University Press, 2001), 20; McDonough, *War in Kentucky*, 42; Robert C. Black III, *The*

Railroads of the Confederacy (Chapel Hill: University of North Carolina Press, 1998), xxvii; Thomas Weber, *The Northern Railroads in the Civil War: 1861–1865* (Bloomington: Indiana University Press, 1952), 205.

4. McDonough, *War in Kentucky*, 35.

5. Ibid., 33; Bruce Catton, *Grant Moves South* (Boston: Little, Brown, 1960), 280.

6. McDonough, *War in Kentucky*, 36.

7. Kenneth W. Noe, *Perryville: This Grand Havoc of Battle* (Lexington: University Press of Kentucky, 2001), 24.

8. Ibid., 24–25; McDonough, *War in Kentucky*, 36.

9. McDonough, *War in Kentucky*, 40.

10. Connelly, *Army of the Heartland*, 175.

11. Stanley F. Horn, *The Army of Tennessee* (Norman: University of Oklahoma Press, 1941), 160.

12. Noe, *Perryville*, 24–25; McDonough, *War in Kentucky*, 32–33.

13. US War Department, *The War of the Rebellion: A Compilation of the Official Records of the Union and Confederate Armies*, 128 vols. (Washington, DC: US Government Printing Office, 1880–1901), vol. 17, 2:601 (hereafter referred to as *OR*); Noe, *Perryville*, 21.

14. Ezra J. Warner, *Generals in Gray: Lives of the Confederate Commanders* (Baton Rouge: Louisiana State University Press, 1959), 30–31; Horn, *Army of Tennessee*, 153–54.

15. Horn, *Army of Tennessee*, 72–73; Warner, *Generals in Gray*, 22–23.

16. Warner, *Generals in Gray*, 30–31.

17. Ibid., xxiv, 62–63.

18. *OR*, vol. 17, 2:614; McDonough, *War in Kentucky*, 1–8.

19. Earl J. Hess, *Braxton Bragg: The Most Hated Man of the Confederacy* (Chapel Hill: University of North Carolina Press, 2016), 51; Horn, *Army of Tennessee*, 230.

20. Hess, *Braxton Bragg*, 80–85.

21. Richard M. McMurry, *Two Great Rebel Armies: An Essay in Confederate Military History* (Chapel Hill: University of North Carolina Press, 1989), 110–17.

22. Warner, *Generals in Gray*, 279–80. For a detailed biography of Kirby Smith, see Joseph H. Parks, *General Edmund Kirby Smith, C.S.A.* (Baton Rouge: Louisiana State University Press, 1982). Apparently, the use

of the name Kirby differentiated the general from other Smiths within the military. During his lifetime his name was not hyphenated Kirby-Smith, and that stance is utilized here. Parks, *General Edmond Kirby Smith*, 117–19n5. Noe, *Perryville*, 27; *OR*, vol. 5, 1073; *OR*, vol. 7, 908.

23. McDonough, *War in Kentucky*, 40, 68–70; Kenneth A. Hafendorfer, *The Battle of Richmond, Kentucky: August 30, 1862* (Louisville: KH Press, 2006), 3.

24. McDonough, *War in Kentucky*, 32–33.

25. *OR*, vol. 16, 2:734–35; Noe, *Perryville*, 29.

26. Noe, *Perryville*, 29.

27. Ibid.

28. *OR*, vol. 16, 2:745–46; *OR*, vol. 17, 2:619, 627; Thomas Lawrence Connelly and Archer Jones, *The Politics of Command: Factions and Ideas in Confederate Strategy* (Baton Rouge: Louisiana State University Press, 1973) 106–7; Connelly, *Army of the Heartland*, 206–7; William C. Davis, *Jefferson Davis: The Man and His Hour* (Baton Rouge: Louisiana State University Press, 1991), 406; Noe, *Perryville*, 33.

29. *OR*, vol. 16, 2:745–46; Noe, *Perryville*, 33.

30. *OR*, vol. 16, 2:733–34; *OR*, vol. 16, 1:768–70; Noe, *Perryville*, 31; Mc-Donough, *War in Kentucky*, 79; Connelly, *Army of the Heartland*, 195.

31. Noe, *Perryville*, 28, 68.

32. Ibid., 31–32.

33. Ibid., 28–29.

34. Ibid., 31–32.

35. *OR*, vol. 16, 1:1088–89; Earl J. Hess, *The Civil War in the West: Victory and Defeat from the Appalachians to the Mississippi* (Chapel Hill: University of North Carolina Press, 2012), 94.

36. Noe, *Perryville*, 33; McDonough, *War in Kentucky*, 78–80.

37. Noe, *Perryville*, 100–102; McDonough, *War in Kentucky*, 307–8.

38. Noe, *Perryville*, 100–102; McDonough, *War in Kentucky*, 307–8.

39. Ezra J. Warner, *Generals in Blue: Lives of the Union Commanders* (Baton Rouge: Louisiana State University, 1964), 51-52.

40. Hess, *Civil War in the West*, 94; McDonough, *War in Kentucky*, 69.

41. McDonough, *War in Kentucky*, 38.

42. Ibid., 69–70.

43. Ibid., 71.

44. Ibid., 74.

45. Ibid., 74.

46. Ibid., 74–75; Noe, *Perryville*, 30; Hess, *Civil War in the West*, 94.

47. Connelly, *Army of the Heartland*, 198–200.

48. *OR*, vol. 16, 2:104; Noe, *Perryville*, 47.

49. McDonough, *War in Kentucky*, 77; Noe, *Perryville*, 31–33.

50. Noe, *Perryville*, 32–33.

51. *OR*, vol. 16, 2:734–35; McDonough, *War in Kentucky*, 77.

52. Noe, *Perryville*, 33.

53. Ibid.

54. Ibid.

55. Peterson, *Confederate Combat Commander*, 83.

56. Noe, *Perryville*, 32, 37.

57. McDonough, *War in Kentucky*, 320.

Chapter 2. The Kentucky Campaign Begins, August 1–29, 1862

1. *OR*, vol. 16, 2:748; McDonough, *War in Kentucky*, 77–82.

2. *OR*, vol. 16, 2:733–34.

3. Ibid., 748–49, 751–53; McDonough, *War in Kentucky*, 80–81; Noe, *Perryville*, 32–33.

4. *OR*, vol. 16, 2:752–53; Noe, *Perryville*, 34.

5. *OR*, vol. 16, 2:752–53.

6. Ibid.

7. Ibid.; Noe, *Perryville*, 34; Connelly, *Army of the Heartland*, 209–10.

8. Connelly, *Army of the Heartland*, 209–10; Hafendorfer, *The Battle of Richmond, Kentucky: August 30, 1862* (Louisville: KH Press, 2006), 8, 17–20.

9. McDonough, *War in Kentucky*, 84–85; Noe, *Perryville*, 36–39.

10. Clark, *Railroads in the Civil War*, 20.

11. McDonough, *War in Kentucky*, 45.

12. Ibid., 55–57; Michael R. Bradley, *The Raiding Winter* (Gretna, LA: Pelican, 2013), 33; Warner, *Generals in Gray*, 220–21.

13. Hafendorfer, *Battle of Richmond, Kentucky*, 404–5n35.

14. Ibid., 8, 73.

15. McDonough, *War in Kentucky*, 37.

16. Ibid.; Earl J. Hess, *Banners to the Breeze: The Kentucky Campaign, Corinth and Stones River* (Lincoln: University of Nebraska Press, 2000), 12.

17. *OR*, vol. 16, 1:843–44, 857; McDonough, *War in Kentucky*, 57–59; Hafendorfer, *Battle of Richmond, Kentucky*, 17; Noe, *Perryville*, 46–47 (note that Noe erroneously dates the event August 10); Hess, *Banners to the Breeze*, 12.

18. *OR*, vol. 16, 1:398, 445, 451; McDonough, *War in Kentucky*, 88, 104–13; Noe, *Perryville*, 59–61; Hess, *Banners to the Breeze*, 58–61.

19. Hess, *Banners to the Breeze*, 57.

20. Noe, *Perryville*, 46–47; McDonough, *War in Kentucky*, 45.

21. *OR*, vol. 16, 2:344, 352.

22. Ibid., 348; Hafendorfer, *Battle of Richmond, Kentucky*, 32.

23. *OR*, vol. 16, 2:351, 404.

24. Ibid., 405.

25. Ibid, 435–36; Hafendorfer, *Battle of Richmond, Kentucky*, 65–66.

26. *OR*, vol. 16, 2:435–36; Hafendorfer, *Battle of Richmond, Kentucky*, 65–66.

27. *OR*, vol. 16, 2:435–36; Hafendorfer, *Battle of Richmond, Kentucky*, 65–66.

28. *OR*, vol. 16, 2:435–36; Hafendorfer, *Battle of Richmond, Kentucky*, 65–66.

29. Lew Wallace, *Lew Wallace: An Autobiography* (1906; repr., Harrisburg, PA: Archive Society, 1997), 2:597; Hafendorfer, *Battle of Richmond, Kentucky*, 38.

30. Hafendorfer, *Battle of Richmond, Kentucky*, 66.

31. Ibid; *OR*, vol. 16, 2:448.

32. Hafendorfer, *Battle of Richmond, Kentucky*, 71.

33. Ibid., 152.

34. Wallace had been "demoted" to commander of a regiment after Maj. Gen. Ulysses S. Grant's deemed him too tardy in arriving on the Shiloh battlefield. Wallace was briefly in command of troops sent to oppose Kirby Smith. He led the Union Army of Kentucky for three days. Wallace, *Lew Wallace*, 597; Hafendorfer, *Battle of Richmond, Kentucky*, 38, 44–52.

35. *OR*, vol. 16, 2:753; Hafendorfer, *Battle of Richmond, Kentucky*, 43.

36. Hafendorfer, *Battle of Richmond, Kentucky*, 43; Mapquest, *Kentucky*.

37. *OR*, vol. 16, 2:751, 753.

38. Ibid., 766.

39. Ibid., 780; Warren D. Lambert, *When the Ripe Pears Fell: The Battle of Richmond, Kentucky* (Richmond, KY: Madison County Historical Society, 1995), 40–41.

40. *OR*, vol. 16, 1:944; Hafendorfer, *Battle of Richmond, Kentucky*, 86–102; Lambert, *When the Ripe Pears Fell*, 48–54.

41. Hafendorfer, *Battle of Richmond, Kentucky*, 38; Wallace, *Lew Wallace: An Autobiography*, 597.

42. *OR*, vol. 16, 2:784; Noe, *Perryville*, 36; Connelly, *Army of the Heartland*, 222.

43. Noe, *Perryville*, 51, 58–59.

44. *OR*, vol. 16, 2:296–97; Larry J. Daniel, *Days of Glory: The Army of the Cumberland, 1861–1865* (Baton Rouge: Louisiana State University Press, 2004), 107–8; Hess, *Civil War in the West*, 98; Noe, *Perryville*, 51.

45. *OR*, vol. 16, 2:13–14; Noe, *Perryville*, 58–59; Connelly, *Army of the Heartland*, 221–22; McDonough, *War in Kentucky*, 111–12.

46. J. Stoddard Johnston, *Memoranda of Facts Bearing on General Bragg's Kentucky Campaign, January 8, 1863* (Louisville: Filson Club Historical Society. Manuscript in J. Stoddard Johnston Military Papers); McDonough, *War in Kentucky*, 184–85; Connelly, *Army of the Heartland*, 221–25.

47. Noe, *Perryville*, 59; McDonough, *War in Kentucky*, 113; Connelly, *Army of the Heartland*, 225.

48. *OR*, vol. 16, 2:876; Noe, *Perryville*, 102.

49. Connelly, *Army of the Heartland*, 222.

Chapter 3. The Battle of Richmond, Kentucky, August 30, 1862

1. *OR*, vol. 16, 1:918–19; Hafendorfer, *Battle of Richmond, Kentucky*, 41, 71.

2. *OR*, vol. 16, 1:911; Hafendorfer, *Battle of Richmond, Kentucky*, 86; Wallace, *Lew Wallace*, 597.

3. Hafendorfer, *Battle of Richmond, Kentucky*, 40.

4. Ibid., 86; *OR*, vol. 16, 1:911.

5. Hafendorfer, *Battle of Richmond, Kentucky*, 38–40.

6. Ibid., 86; *OR*, vol. 16, 1:911; Lambert, *When the Ripe Pears Fell*, 58. There is controversy as to whether Manson was ever officially ordered to utilize the Kentucky River as a defensive position. See McDonough, *War in Kentucky*, 118.

7. *OR*, vol. 16, 1:911; Hafendorfer, *Battle of Richmond, Kentucky*, 86; Lambert, *When the Ripe Pears Fell*, 58–59.

8. *OR*, vol. 16, 1:909; Hafendorfer, *Battle of Richmond, Kentucky*, 38–40; McDonough, *War in Kentucky*, 118–20.

9. *OR*, vol. 16, 1:949–50; Hafendorfer, *Battle of Richmond, Kentucky*, 116, 121; Lambert, *When the Ripe Pears Fell*, 67.

10. Hafendorfer, *Battle of Richmond, Kentucky*, 8, 115, 118, 137; Warner, *Generals in Gray*, 280.

11. *OR*, vol. 16, 1:944–45; Hafendorfer, *Battle of Richmond, Kentucky* 104–5, 109; Lambert, *When the Ripe Pears Fell*, 51.

12. *OR*, vol. 16, 1:934, 950; Lambert, *When the Ripe Pears Fell*, 62–68.

13. *OR*, vol. 16, 1:934; Lambert, *When the Ripe Pears Fell*, 68.

14. *OR*, vol. 16, 1:942; Lambert, *When the Ripe Pears Fell*, 69.

15. *OR*, vol. 16, 1:945; Lambert, *When the Ripe Pears Fell*, 74, 78.

16. *OR*, vol. 16, 1:947, 950; Lambert, *When the Ripe Pears Fell*, 62.

17. *OR*, vol. 16, 1:940, 942, 945–46; Hafendorfer, *Battle of Richmond, Kentucky*, 144–45, 152–53.

18. Christopher Perello, *The Quest for Annihilation: The Role & Mechanics of Battle in the American Civil War* (Bakersfield, CA: Strategy & Tactics Press, 2009), 77–78, 99.

19. *OR*, vol. 16, 1:942, 945; Hafendorfer, *Battle of Richmond, Kentucky*, 144–97; Lambert, *When the Ripe Pears Fell*, 120.

20. Stuart W. Sanders, "To Hell or to Victory: Confederate General Alfred J. Vaughan Jr.," in editors, *Confederate Generals in the Western Theater: Essays on America's Civil War*, ed. Lawrence Lee Hewitt and Arthur W. Bergeron Jr. (Knoxville: University of Tennessee Press, 2010), 2:32.

21. Lambert, *When the Ripe Pears Fell*, 68.

22. Ibid., 119–22.

23. Hafendorfer, *Battle of Richmond, Kentucky*, 209–19.

24. Ibid., 184.

25. Ibid.

26. Ibid.

27. Ibid.

28. *OR*, vol. 16, 1:925, 938; Hafendorfer, *Battle of Richmond, Kentucky*, 184, 295–98.

29. *OR*, vol. 16, 1:925, 938; Hafendorfer, *Battle of Richmond, Kentucky*, 295–308.

30. *OR*, vol. 16, 1:908–9; Lambert, *When the Ripe Pears Fell*, 134.

31. *OR*, vol. 16, 1:925, 938; Hafendorfer, *Battle of Richmond, Kentucky*, 297.

32. Lambert, *When the Ripe Pears Fell*, 158.

Chapter 4. The Kentucky Campaign Continues, August 31–October 7, 1862

1. McDonough, *War in Kentucky*, 104–10; Hess, *Banners to the Breeze*, 13.

2. Noe, *Perryville*, 30; Clark, *Railroads in the Civil War*, 30.

3. McDonough, *War in Kentucky*, 106; Nathaniel C. Hughes Jr., *General William J. Hardee: Old Reliable* (Baton Rouge: Louisiana State University Press, 1965), 121.

4. *OR*, vol. 16, 2:451; McDonough, *War in Kentucky*, 110–12.

5. *OR*, vol. 16, 2:451; McDonough, *War in Kentucky*, 110–12.

6. *OR*, vol. 16, 2:451; McDonough, *War in Kentucky*, 110–12.

7. *OR*, vol. 16, 2:451; McDonough, *War in Kentucky*, 110–12; Noe, *Perryville*, 58–59.

8. *OR*, vol. 16, 2:451; McDonough, *War in Kentucky*, 110–12; Noe, *Perryville*, 58–59.

9. *OR*, vol. 16, 2:470; Noe, *Perryville*, 61–62.

10. *OR*, vol. 16, 1:17; Connelly, *Army of the Heartland*, 228–29.

11. *OR*, vol. 16, 1:974–78; Noe, *Perryville*, 69–70; Horn, *Army of Tennessee*, 168; Hal Engerud, *The Battle of Munfordville: September 14th–17th, 1862* (Munfordville, KY: Hart County Historical Society, 1994), 3.

12. *OR*, vol. 16, 1:980; Noe, *Perryville*, 69–70.

13. *OR*, vol. 16, 1:980; Noe, *Perryville*, 69–70.

14. Connelly, *Army of the Heartland*, 228. The railroad bridge at Munfordville was "a marvel of civil engineering" per Hess, *Banners to the Breeze*, 63. According to Noe, *Perryville*, 68, the bridge was 1,800 feet long and 115 feet above the Green River.

15. Noe, *Perryville*, 70.

16. Ibid.

17. *OR*, vol. 16, 1:962, 968.

18. Ibid.; Hess, *Banners to the Breeze*, 66–69; McDonough, *War in Kentucky*, 172–81; Noe, *Perryville*, 70–71.

19. Connelly, *Army of the Heartland*, 228–34; Noe, *Perryville*, 73–74; Hess, *Banners to the Breeze*, 69–70.

20. Noe, *Perryville*, 73.

21. Ibid., 76.

22. Noe, *Perryville*, 76; McDonough, *War in Kentucky*, 184.

23. *OR*, vol. 16, 2:843; McDonough, *War in Kentucky*, 183; Horn, *Army of Tennessee*, 170–72.

24. *OR*, vol. 16, 1:1091; *OR*, vol. 16, 2:830; McDonough, *War in Kentucky*, 185.

25. *OR*, vol. 16, 1:1091; McDonough, *War in Kentucky*, 185.

26. *OR*, vol. 16, 2:843; McDonough, *War in Kentucky*, 183; Horn, *Army of Tennessee*, 170–72; Noe, *Perryville*, 76; Kirby Smith to J. Stoddard Johnston, 31 October 1866, Johnston Papers, Filson.

27. McDonough, *War in Kentucky*, 184; Horn, *Army of Tennessee*, 172.

28. McDonough, *War in Kentucky*, 184; Horn, *Army of Tennessee*, 172; *OR*, vol. 16, 2:849.

29. Horn, *Army of Tennessee*, 176–77; McDonough, *War in Kentucky*, 186–87.

30. Noe, *Perryville*, 73, 89–92.

31. McDonough, *War in Kentucky*, 189; Horn, *Army of Tennessee*, 172; Connelly, *Army of the Heartland*, 234.

32. Horn, *Army of Tennessee*, 170–72; McDonough, *War in Kentucky*, 200.

33. McDonough, *War in Kentucky*, 193; Noe, *Perryville*, 92.

34. McDonough, *War in Kentucky*, 193; Noe, *Perryville*, 92.

35. Noe, *Perryville*, 93; McDonough, *War in Kentucky*, 195.

36. *OR*, vol. 16, 2:539, 555; Noe, *Perryville*, 95–97; Horn, *Army of Tennessee*, 176.

37. Noe, *Perryville*, 97.

38. Ibid.; Warner, *Generals in Blue*, 424–25.

39. Noe, *Perryville*, 97–98; Warner, *Generals in Blue*, 173–74; Daniel, *Days of Glory*, 137.

40. Noe, *Perryville*, 97–98; Warner, *Generals in Blue*, 173–74; Daniel, *Days of Glory*, 137.

41. Noe, *Perryville*, 98.

42. *OR*, vol. 16, 1:283; McDonough, *War in Kentucky*, 267–70.

43. Kenneth A. Hafendorfer, *Perryville: Battle for Kentucky* (Louisville: KH Press, 1991), 288; Noe, *Perryville*, 234–35.

44. Kenneth A. Hafendorfer, *Perryville: Battle for Kentucky* (Louisville: KH Press, 1991), 288; Noe, *Perryville*, 234–35.

45. *OR*, vol. 16, 2:733–34; Noe, *Perryville*, 31–32, 39–40.

46. *OR*, vol. 16, 2:846; Noe, *Perryville*, 103.

47. Noe, *Perryville*, 73.

48. Ibid., 104.

49. Ibid.

50. Ibid.

51. Ibid.

52. *OR*, vol. 16, 2:886; Noe, *Perryville*, 104–5.

53. Noe, *Perryville*, 105.

54. Ibid.

55. *OR*, vol. 16, 2:372; Noe, *Perryville*, 89; McDonough, *War in Kentucky*, 190–92.

56. *OR*, vol. 16, 2:538–39; Noe, *Perryville*, 94.

57. *OR*, vol. 16, 2:555; Noe, *Perryville*, 94.

58. Noe, *Perryville*, 94.

59. *OR*, vol. 16, 2:538; Noe, *Perryville*, 94.

60. Noe, *Perryville*, 112.

61. Ibid.

62. Ibid., 90–92; Hafendorfer, *Perryville*, 66.

63. Ibid., 125.

64. Warner, *Generals in Blue*, 501.

65. Noe, *Perryville*, 231–33.

66. Conjecture by the author: Thomas seemed to be more sensitive to the administration's desires.

67. Connelly, *Army of the Heartland*, 241.

68. Ibid.

69. Ibid., 241–42.

70. Ibid.

71. Ibid.

72. Ibid. 245; McDonough, *War in Kentucky*, 200; Noe, *Perryville*, 128–29.

73. Noe, *Perryville*, 128–29; Horn, *Army of Tennessee*, 178.

74. Hess, *Banners to the Breeze*, 91; McDonough, *War in Kentucky*, 200; Noe, *Perryville*, 129.

75. Noe, *Perryville*, 129–30.

76. Ibid.

Chapter 5. The Battle of Perryville, October 8, 1862

1. Noe, *Perryville*, 106.

2. Ibid., 113–21; McDonough, *War in Kentucky*, 206–8.

3. Noe, *Perryville*, 112, 125–26.

4. *OR*, vol. 16, 1:1095; Noe, *Perryville*, 132.

5. Noe, *Perryville*, 130.

6. Ibid., 130; *OR*, vol. 16, 2:915; Hess, *Banners to the Breeze*, 83.

7. Hess, *Banners to the Breeze*, 82; Connelly, *Army of the Heartland*, 240.

8. Connelly, *Army of the Heartland*, 242; Horn, *Army of Tennessee*, 178.

9. Hess, *Banners to the Breeze*, 83–85; Hafendorfer, *Perryville*, 98; McDonough, *War in Kentucky*, 203–4.

10. *OR*, vol. 16, 2:578–79; Hafendorfer, *Perryville*, 98–99; Noe, *Perryville*, 131–33.

11. *OR*, vol. 16, 1:1095; Connelly, *Army of the Heartland*, 256–57; Noe, *Perryville*, 132.

12. *OR*, vol. 16, 1:89, 525, 665; 112–23; *OR*, vol. 16, 2:560–61; Noe, *Perryville*, 112–23.

13. *OR*, vol. 16, 1:1024; Noe, *Perryville*, 119–20, 122; Connelly, *Army of the Heartland*, 256; McDonough, *War in Kentucky*, 203.

14. Noe, *Perryville*, 117.

15. Ibid., 118, 120–21.

16. Ibid., 133.

17. Ibid., 168–69.

18. Hafendorfer, *Perryville*, 160; Noe, *Perryville*, 168.

19. Hess, *Banners to the Breeze*, 91.

20. Ibid., 87; Noe, *Perryville*, 168.

21. Hess, *Banners to the Breeze*, 88.

22. Ibid., 91.

23. *OR*, vol. 16, 1:1088, 1091; Noe, *Perryville*, 313–14; Hafendorfer, *Perryville*, 389–90.

24. Hafendorfer, *Perryville*, 390; Noe, *Perryville*, 313.

25. Noe, *Perryville*, 169.

26. *OR*, vol. 16, 1:1099; Braxton Bragg, (Cleveland: Western Reserve Historical Society), *Hardee to Bragg, October 7, 1862, 7:30 p.m.*; Noe, *Perryville*, 139–40, 170; Hafendorfer, *Perryville*, 127.

27. *OR*, vol. 16, 1:1092; Joseph H. Parks, *General Leonidas Polk, C.S.A.: The Fighting Bishop* (Baton Rouge: Louisiana State University Press, 1990), 222; Noe, *Perryville*, 170.

28. *OR*, vol. 16, 1:1092; Noe, *Perryville*, 170–71; Hafendorfer, *Perryville*, 162–63.

29. Hafendorfer, *Perryville*, 163.

30. *OR*, vol. 16, 1:1092; Hafendorfer, *Perryville*, 163–64.

31. *Confederate Veteran* (Nashville: 1908), 16:225; Hafendorfer, *Perryville*, 162.

32. Noe, *Perryville*, 171–72.

33. Hafendorfer, *Perryville*, 164–65, 198, 206, 217, 228. For a brief review of the Battle of Perryville, see McDonough, *War in Kentucky*, 243–87.

34. Noe, *Perryville*, 215, 421n6.

35. Hafendorfer, *Perryville*, 228. Hafendorfer posits that had Bull Nelson would surely have taken part in the fighting.

36. Ibid., 321, 389; Noe, *Perryville*, 313.

37. Noe, *Perryville*, 313.

38. Ibid., 313–14; McDonough, *War in Kentucky*, 305.

39. Noe, *Perryville*, 313–14; McDonough, *War in Kentucky*, 305.

40. Noe, *Perryville*, 313–14; McDonough, *War in Kentucky*, 305.

41. Noe, *Perryville*, 313–14; McDonough, *War in Kentucky*, 305.

42. *OR*, vol. 16, 1:1088, 1093, 1095; McDonough, *War in Kentucky*, 305; Hafendorfer, *Perryville*, 390; Noe, *Perryville*, 314; Connelly, *Army of the Heartland*, 267.

43. Hafendorfer, *Perryville*, 399–400; Noe, *Perryville*, 315.

44. Noe, *Perryville*, 315–16.

Chapter 6. Retreat Out of Kentucky, October 9–24, 1862

1. Hess, *Banners to the Breeze*, 108–10; Noe, *Perryville*, 329, 333; McDonough, *War in Kentucky*, 305–8.

2. Stuart W. Sanders, "A Name Worth a Division: Simon Bolivar Buckner and the 1862 Kentucky Campaign," in *Confederate Generals in the Western Theater: Essays on America's Civil War*, ed. Lawrence Lee Hewitt and Arthur W. Bergeron (Knoxville: University of Tennessee Press, 2011), 3:127–29.

3. Noe, *Perryville*, 334–35; Connelly, *Army of the Heartland*, 269–70.

4. Noe, *Perryville*, 334; Hess, *Banners to the Breeze*, 110.

5. *OR*, vol. 16, 1:1088, 1093. Note that Bragg now proclaimed he had twenty thousand rifles for recruits. Noe, *Perryville*, 334; Connelly, *Army of the Heartland*, 272–79.

6. *OR*, vol. 16, 1:1088, 1093; Noe, *Perryville*, 334; Connelly, *Army of the Heartland*, 272–79.

7. *OR*, vol. 16, 1:1093; Connelly, *Army of the Heartland*, 279–80.

8. Noe, *Perryville*, 337–39; Hess, *Banners to the Breeze*, 112.

9. Noe, *Perryville*, 337; Connelly, *Army of the Heartland*, 279–80; Sam Watkins, *Company Aytch or, a Side Show of the Big Show and Other Sketches*, ed. M. Thomas Inge (1882; repr., New York: Penguin Books, 1999), 50.

10. Noe, *Perryville*, 337; Hess, *Banners to the Breeze*, 112–13.

11. Hess, *Banners to the Breeze*, 120; McDonough, *War in Kentucky*, 311, 314; Peter Cozzens, *No Better Place to Die: The Battle of Stones River* (Chicago: University of Illinois Press, 1991), 8, 11, 83.

12. Connelly, *Army of the Heartland*, 277.

13. Hess, *Banners to the Breeze*, 112.

14. *OR*, vol. 16, 2:612; Hess, *Banners to the Breeze*, 112; Noe, *Perryville*, 340.

15. Noe, *Perryville*, 340.

16. Ibid. 340–41.

17. Ibid., 340–42.

18. *OR*, vol. 16, 2:619; Noe, *Perryville*, 341–43.

19. Daniel, *Days of Glory*, 177; Hess, *Banners to the Breeze*, 117–18.

20. Cozzens, *No Better Place to Die*, 19–28.

21. Noe, *Perryville*, 341.

Chapter 7. Aftermath and Conclusions

1. Noe, *Perryville*, 339.

2. Cozzens, *No Better Place to Die*, 38.

3. Noe, *Perryville*, 338–39.

4. Ibid., 339–43.

5. Ibid., 334; Michael B. Ballard, *Vicksburg: The Campaign That Opened the Mississippi* (Chapel Hill: University of North Carolina Press, 2004), 78.

Appendix I. A Driving Tour of the Critical Decisions of the 1862 Kentucky Campaign

1. Noe, *Perryville*, 24.

2. *OR*, vol. 17, 2:614.

3. *OR*, vol. 16, 2:745–46.

4. Ibid., 2:733–34.

5. Noe, *Perryville*, 30.

6. *OR*, vol. 16, 2:741.

7. *OR*, vol. 16, 1:1089.

8. *OR*, vol. 16, 2:416–17.

9. Ibid., 766–67.

10. Ibid.

11. Ibid., 769.

12. Ibid., 435–36.

13. McDonough, *War in Kentucky*, 117–18.

14. Ibid., 121.

15. *OR*, vol. 16, 1:911.

16. Ibid., 1:934.

17. Ibid., 1:938.

18. *OR*, vol. 16, 1:1091.

19. *OR*, vol. 16, 2:904–5.

20. *OR*, vol. 16, 1:1088.

21. *OR*, vol. 16, 2:619.

22. *OR*, vol. 16, 1:1096.

23. Ibid., 1:1110.

24. *OR*, vol. 16, 1:1092

25. Ibid., 1:1093.

26. Noe, *Perryville*, 168–69.

27. The Buell Commission was formed to evaluate Buell's performance during the Kentucky Campaign of 1862, but it was rife with political undertones.

28. Warner, *Generals in Blue*, 174.

29. *OR*, vol. 16, 1:49.

30. Ibid., 1:980.

31. Ibid., 1:968.

32. Ibid., 1:36.

BIBLIOGRAPHY

Primary Sources

Bragg, Braxton. *Hardee to Bragg, October 7, 1862, 7:30 P.M., Papers*. Cleveland: Western Reserve Historical Society.

Confederate Veteran. 40 vols. Nashville: 1893–1932.

Johnston, J. Stoddard. *Memoranda of Facts Bearing on General Bragg's Kentucky Campaign, January 8, 1863*. Louisville: Filson Club Historical Society. Manuscript in J. Stoddard Johnston Military Papers.

Liddell, St. John Richardson. *Liddell's Record: St. John Richardson Liddell: Brigadier General, CSA, Staff Officer and Brigade Commander, Army of Tennessee*. Edited by Nathaniel C. Hughes Jr. Baton Rouge: Louisiana State University Press, 1985.

US War Department. *The War of the Rebellion: A Compilation of the Official Records of the Union and Confederate Armies*. 128 vols. Washington, DC: 1880–1901.

Wallace, Lew. *Lew Wallace: An Autobiography*. 1906. Reprint. Harrisburg, PA: Archive Society, 1997.

Watkins, Sam. *Company Aytch or, a Side Show of the Big Show and Other Sketches*. Edited by M. Thomas Inge. 1882. Reprint. New York: Penguin Books, 1999.

Secondary Sources

Ballard, Michael B. *Vicksburg: The Campaign That Opened the Mississippi.* Chapel Hill: University of North Carolina Press, 2004.

Black, Robert C., III. *The Railroads of the Confederacy.* Chapel Hill: University of North Carolina Press, 1998.

Bradley, Michael R. *The Raiding Winter.* Gretna, LA: Pelican, 2013.

Catton, Bruce. *Grant Moves South.* Boston: Little, Brown, 1960.

Connelly, Thomas Lawrence, and Archer Jones. *The Politics of Command: Factions and Ideas in Confederate Strategy.* Baton Rouge: Louisiana State University Press, 1973.

Cozzens, Peter. *No Better Place to Die: The Battle of Stones River.* Chicago: University of Illinois Press, 1991.

Daniel, Larry J. *Days of Glory: The Army of the Cumberland, 1861–1865.* Baton Rouge: Louisiana State University Press, 2004.

Davis, William C. *Jefferson Davis: The Man and His Hour.* Baton Rouge: Louisiana State University Press, 1991.

Engerud, Hal. *The Battle of Munfordville: September 14th–17th, 1862.* Munfordville, KY: Hart County Historical Society, 1994.

Hafendorfer, Kenneth A. *Perryville: Battle for Kentucky.* Louisville: KH Press, 1991.

———. *The Battle of Richmond, Kentucky: August 30, 1862.* Louisville: KH Press, 2006.

Hess, Earl J. *Banners to the Breeze: The Kentucky Campaign, Corinth and Stones River.* Lincoln: University of Nebraska Press, 2000.

———. *Braxton Bragg: The Most Hated Man of the Confederacy.* Chapel Hill: University of North Carolina Press, 2016.

———. *The Civil War in the West: Victory and Defeat from the Appalachians to the Mississippi.* Chapel Hill: University of North Carolina Press, 2012.

Hewitt, Lawrence Lee, and Arthur W. Bergeron Jr., eds. *Confederate Generals in the Western Theater: Classic Essays on America's Civil War, Vol. 1.* Knoxville: University of Tennessee Press, 2010.

———, eds. *Confederate Generals in the Western Theater: Essays on America's Civil War, Vol. 2.* Knoxville: University of Tennessee Press, 2010.

———, eds. *Confederate Generals in the Western Theater: Essays on America's Civil War, Vol. 3.* Knoxville: University of Tennessee Press, 2011.

Hewitt, Lawrence L., Arthur W. Bergeron Jr., and Thomas E. Schott, eds. *Confederate Generals in the Trans-Mississippi, Vol. 1*. Knoxville: University of Tennessee Press, 2013.

Holman, Kurt. *Battle of Perryville: Movement Maps Showing the Fighting Ground of the Union Left and Centre, 12:00 P.M. to 8:00 P.M.* Perryville, KY: Friends of Perryville Battlefield, 2016.

Horn, Stanley F. *The Army of Tennessee*. Norman: University of Oklahoma Press, 1941.

Hughes, Nathaniel C., Jr. *General William J. Hardee: Old Reliable*. Baton Rouge: Louisiana State University Press, 1965.

Lambert, D. Warren. *When the Ripe Pears Fell: The Battle of Richmond, Kentucky*. Richmond, KY: Madison County Historical Society, 1995.

McDonough, James Lee. *Stones River: Bloody Winter in Tennessee*. Knoxville: University of Tennessee Press, 1980.

———. *War in Kentucky: From Shiloh to Perryville*. Knoxville: University of Tennessee Press, 1994.

McMurry, Richard M. *Two Great Rebel Armies: An Essay in Confederate Military History*. Chapel Hill: University of North Carolina Press, 1989.

McWhiney, Grady. *Braxton Bragg and Confederate Defeat, Vol. I*. Tuscaloosa: University of Alabama Press, 1969.

Musicant, Ivan. *Divided Waters: The Naval History of the Civil War*. Edison, NJ: Castle Books, 2000.

Noe, Kenneth W. *Perryville: This Grand Havoc of Battle*. Lexington: University Press of Kentucky, 2001.

Parks, Joseph H. *General Edmund Kirby Smith, C.S.A.* Baton Rouge: Louisiana State University Press, 1982.

———. *General Leonidas Polk, C.S.A.: The Fighting Bishop*. Baton Rouge: Louisiana State University Press, 1990.

Perello, Christopher. *The Quest for Annihilation: The Role & Mechanics of Battle in the American Civil War*. Bakersfield, CA: Strategy & Tactics Press, 2009.

Peterson, Lawrence K. *Confederate Combat Commander: The Remarkable Life of Brigadier General Alfred Jefferson Vaughan Jr.* Knoxville: University of Tennessee Press, 2013.

Spruill, Matt, and Lee Spruill. *Winter Lightning: A Guide to the Battle of Stones River*. Knoxville: University of Tennessee Press, 2013.

Stoker, Donald. *The Grand Design: Strategy and the U.S. Civil War.* New York: Oxford University Press, 2010.

Warner, Ezra J. *Generals in Blue: Lives of the Union Commanders.* Baton Rouge: Louisiana State University Press, 1964.

————. *Generals in Gray: Lives of the Confederate Commanders.* Baton Rouge: Louisiana State University Press, 1959.

Weber, Thomas. *The Northern Railroads in the Civil War: 1861–1865.* Bloomington: Indiana University Press, 1952.

Woodworth, Steven E. *Decision in the Heartland: The Civil War in the West.* Westport, CT: Praeger, 2008.

————. *Jefferson Davis and His Generals: The Failure of Confederate Command in the West.* Lawrence: University Press of Kansas, 1990.

INDEX